Inner Healing Deliverance & Restoration

A Workbook for the Spiritually Broken

Inner Healing Deliverance & Restoration

Dr. Sun Fannin

Inner Healing Deliverance & Restoration: A Workbook for the Spiritually Broken

Copyright © 2025 Dr. Sun Fannin

Softcover ISBN: 978-1-950880-89-8
eBook ISBN: 978-1-950880-91-1

Scripture quotations from The Authorized (King James) Version. Rights in the Authorized Version in the United Kingdom are vested in the Crown. Reproduced by permission of the Crown's patentee, Cambridge University Press.

Scripture quotations taken from the Amplified® Bible (AMP), Copyright © 2015 by The Lockman Foundation Used by permission. www.Lockman.org

Scripture taken from the HOLY BIBLE, NEW INTERNATIONAL VERSION®. Copyright © 1973, 1978, 1984 Biblica. Used by permission of Zondervan. All rights reserved. The "NIV" and "New International Version" trademarks are registered in the United States Patent and Trademark Office by Biblica.

Scripture taken from the New King James Version®. Copyright © 1982 by Thomas Nelson, Inc. Used by permission. All rights reserved.

All rights reserved. No part of this book may be reproduced or transmitted in any form or by any means, electronic or mechanical, includ ing photocopying, recording or by any information storage and retrieval system, without permission in writing from the copyright owner. For information on distribution rights, royalties, derivative works or licens ing opportunities on behalf of this content or work, please contact the publisher at the address below

Cover design by AuthorSource Media
Typeset by Medlar Publishing Solutions Pvt Ltd, India.

TABLE OF CONTENTS

Chapter 1	Inner Healing & Restoration	1
Chapter 2	What is Restoration?	7
Chapter 3	God's Vision for Me	11
Chapter 4	The Voice of God	21
Chapter 5	Those Who Hear God's Voice	31
Chapter 6	Healing for the Root of Bitterness	41
Chapter 7	Healing the Wounded Soul	51
Chapter 8	Freedom from an Unforgiving Heart	61
Chapter 9	Breaking Soul Ties	69
Chapter 10	The Power of the Lie	79
Chapter 11	Unbelief and Faith	87
Chapter 12	Discovering Your Self-Worth in Christ	97
Chapter 13	Useful Guidelines for Inner Healing Ministers	103
Chapter 14	Useful Guidelines for Ministering Deliverance	107
Chapter 15	Demon Possession and Christians	113
Chapter 16	How to Maintain Inner Healing and Deliverance	115
	A Note to My Readers	*119*
	Acknowledgements	*121*
	About the Author	*123*

CHAPTER 1

INNER HEALING & RESTORATION

Man Is a Triune Being

Man is created with three distinct parts: body, soul, and spirit. While separating body from soul and spirit is easily understood, Christians have a harder time, when it comes to understanding the difference between spirit and soul. However, the following scriptures show that the spirit and soul are not one in the same.

> *"For the word of God is alive and active. Sharper than any double-edged sword, it penetrates even to dividing soul and spirit, joints, and marrow; it judges the thoughts and attitudes of the heart."*
>
> (Hebrews 4:12)

> *"May God himself, the God of peace, sanctify you through and through. May your whole spirit, soul and body be kept blameless at the coming of our Lord Jesus Christ."*
>
> (1 Thessalonians 5:23)

The Three Parts of Man

Body

The body deals with the physical world, the environment. The human body is like a building that a man occupies.[1] The body is the "house" in which the spirit and soul reside. It is what identifies each person as a unique individual with a distinct appearance.

---

[1] The word "man" is used in a general sense to include all of mankind.

Spirit

The spirit is the inner being, invisible and hidden. For a man to believe in Jesus Christ is to have his spirit reborn or born again (John 3:3). The regenerated[2] spirit of man communicates with God by becoming aware of Him and getting to know His voice and His leading. Man's spirit interacts with the spiritual world. The essence of man is not his body, but his spirit. Paul stresses that the spirit is the center of and the foundation of man: "Don't you know that you yourselves are God's temple and that God's Spirit dwells in your midst?" (1 Corinthians 3:16, NIV). The spirit of a believer who has been born again resides in the light of God as the new creation of Christ (2 Corinthians 5:17), having moved away from darkness (1 John 1:7).

Soul

The soul consists of the mind, will, and emotions, and houses the psychological nature of man. The human soul is in a constant state of transformation through healing and restoration (1 Thessalonians 5:23), and during this process the soul often acts against the will of the Holy Spirit, due to the wounds it has experienced. God wants man to live righteously with his emotions and mind focused on things pleasing to God, exercising his free will according to God's will, and acting out of obedience to the will of God. This happens at deeper levels through receiving inner healing and deliverance. However, the unhealed areas of the soul are vulnerable to the work of evil spirits and their "fiery darts" (Ephesians 6:16).

The soul is a place where all our life's memories are stored, not only the events themselves, but emotions associated with those events. Satan can use traumatic events and the associated emotions to hold man in bondage, so he cannot freely commune with and obey the Holy Spirit.

These emotions have a significant positive or negative impact on man, both psychologically and physically. This is because of the vast realm of the sub-conscious, the place where man's personal experiences are stored. Negative experiences create emotional "scars" on man's soul. In many cases, people are not even aware of their emotional scars; memories are often forgotten or suppressed in their subconscious.

People who have sincerely served God for many years can stop growing suddenly, and their relationship with God starts becoming strained and ultimately detached.

---

[2] "regenerated" refers to the born-again experience. See Jesus' conversation with Nicodemus in John 3.

They are no longer able to praise God and pray, and their communication with Him is no longer free flowing. One day, they discover a bitterness that wells up from within, and they have no clue as to how to deal with their unresolved issues, conflicts, and problems. These are the result of deep, emotional scars that have been locked up in their soul. The truth is, we have all been scarred in one way or another, which is why everyone needs emotional healing and restoration.

God liberates the wounded soul and the oppressed spirit through the power of the Holy Spirit

> *"The Spirit of the Lord is on me, because he has anointed me to proclaim good news to the poor. He has sent me to proclaim freedom for the prisoners and recovery of sight for the blind, to set the oppressed free. To proclaim the year of the Lord's favor."*
>
> (Luke 4:18-19)

He came to heal the wounded spirit

Many Christians are not able to live a life of obedience to the Word of God, due to the hurts and suffering in their soulish realm. Their responses to, and decisions, made based on their circumstances have left damaging wounds in their soul, and the scars have remained in their memories. These memories have chained these people to their past. Jesus came to heal these wounds and to set the captive free.

He came to liberate the prisoners

How a man lives his life is greatly influenced by his ancestors. There are generational curses that affect your emotional makeup or your health. For example, you might know that cancer or heart attacks are part of your ancestral heritage. You might be someone who gets angry quickly, just like your mom or dad.

He came to liberate the oppressed

In this life, people make choices that open the wrong doors, which gives the devil an opportunity to bring oppression and bondage into their lives. These choices include idolatry, fortune telling, superstition, and unwholesome books and movies. They may also include relationships with family and friends who pray to their idols on our behalf.

More often than not, these choices bring us into the bondage of satan's shackles and yokes. These bondages push us further away from the freedom that God desires us to have, and they interfere with the life of blessing and prosperity in Christ that God has planned for us. Through the power of inner healing and deliverance prayer, the Holy Spirit sets us free to live the life God has for us.

One of the most powerful words in the Bible is the word "liberate." God wants us to be free. God wants us to be truly liberated in Christ, breaking free from everything that has been holding us back, including our own memories and emotions.

God wants us to discover who we are in Christ and rejoice in the way He has made us. He wants us to serve Him by loving and serving our families and others, and by freely expressing who He has made us to be.

Regardless of how difficult our life becomes; God wants us to know and understand that in all things He works for the good of those who love Him (Romans 8:28). He wants us to know and enjoy the true freedom that propels us to reach our potential to the fullest and accomplish our goals.

God wants us to be free from our past and any related negativism, and to look to the future with joy in our hearts. He wants us to be able to have joy and serve Him being made able to do His will. But freedom does not come without inner healing. Inner healing allows us to live our lives with joy and frees us from our past. It is the cares of our past that keeps us bound to our hurts.

The word *Christian* means that we are Christ-like in all we do. Just like Jesus, God wants us to follow His commands in our daily lives. Inner healing prayer opens the door to freedom in our souls, so that we can freely serve our Lord.

We learn the love of God through inner healing and restoration

As you receive the love of God, we learn to love and accept ourselves, and also learn to love and accept those around us. Inner healing is a requirement for restoration. Inner healing prayer brings healing and freedom to your soul, so you can love as Jesus wants you to. Part of the requirement for healing is forgiving those who have hurt us in the past. Jesus not only commanded us to love others, but also to forgive them.

Jesus did not ask whether we *want* to forgive, rather He said to *do* it. Determining who is at fault is not important. Instead, freedom follows when we obey the Lord.

God, in all things, works for the good of those who love Him (Romans 8:28). He wants to bring goodness out of everything, even those circumstances that have grieved us.

True forgiveness for yourself and your neighbors heals the wounded emotions and damaging memories stored in your subconscious. Jesus has given us the best possible lesson about forgiveness. Minutes before He died on the cross, Jesus prayed for God to forgive those who had crucified Him. There was no *if* in His request for forgiveness; He did not ask God to forgive them only *if* they changed, or *if* they asked for forgiveness.

Jesus' forgiveness was unconditional

> *Jesus said, "Father, forgive them, for they do not know what they are doing." And they divided up his clothes by casting lots.*
>
> (Luke 23:34)

He said this even though:

- They continued to do Him wrong.
- They refused to change.
- They were not asking for forgiveness.
- They continued to inflict Him pain.
- They continued to hurt Him.

As Jesus shows us, forgiveness *must* be the way of life for the believers. This includes continually forgiving yourself even as God has forgiven you and forgiving others.

CHAPTER 2

WHAT IS RESTORATION?

"I will restore all your leaders as in days of old, your rulers as at the beginning. Afterward you will be called the City of Righteousness, the Faithful City."

(Isaiah 1:26)

The purpose of restoration is:

- To become like it was before, to be established, to be turned back to its original conditions.
- To regain the position lost. Genesis 40:13, the cupbearer regains his position through Joseph interpreting his dreams.
- To regain the function lost. Mark 3:5, Jesus restored a man's withered hands.
- To regain one's authority. 2 Samuel 8:3, King Saul conquered the Kingdom of Zobah and expanded his influence.
- What God wants for the modern church is to regain the power the early church had.

The Meaning of restoration is:

To return our relationship with God to its original conditions. Our spirit has been born again when we accepted Jesus Christ as our Savior, but in our soul realm, all things broken remain broken, i.e., our personality, our character, our speech, our behavior, our attitude. Restoration is the way through which God recreates our relationship with Him, as we live in His grace and as His Word remains in us to transform our lives.

God's intention for mankind:

God intended to show His glory through mankind. He desires to have a relationship with us and to love us, and so that we can love Him in return. When they were sinless, Adam and Eve were "whole" in their spirits and their lives and enjoyed God's company and fellowship with Him. But when Lucifer—the fallen archangel we call the devil or satan, who had betrayed God—transformed himself into a snake, and deceived them into disobeying. Since then, mankind could no longer have a restored relationship with God, which is why Jesus came to this earth.

Adam and Eve, and their sin (See Genesis 3):

Verse 6: tempted by taste and sight (good for food, pleasing to the eye, and also desirable for gaining wisdom)

Verse 6: disobedience (by eating the fruit from the tree of good and evil)

Verse 7: sense of shame (by realizing they were naked)

Verse 8: avoiding God (because of sin)

Verse 10: fearing God

Verses 12-13: Adam blamed Eve, and Eve blamed the snake, instead of admitting to their sin

Verses 14-19: Adam, Eve, and the snake were condemned because of their sins

Verses 21-23: God gave them garments of skin (signifies the coming of Jesus whose blood would cover our injustice and sins) and banished them from the Garden of Eden

After chapter 4: mankind lived a life of fear as their relationship with God was not like before. As a result, Cain grew up to be a man filled with anger, isolation, fear, rebellion, and ended up murdering his own brother Abel.

As God commanded to Adam, God is telling us to:

- To be fruitful and increase in numbers and fill the earth.

> *"God blessed them and said to them, be fruitful and increase in number; fill the earth and subdue it. Rule over the fish in the sea and the birds in the sky and over every living creature that moves on the ground."*
>
> (Genesis 1:28)

- Adam did not obey God.

    "And the LORD God commanded the man, You are free to eat from any tree in the garden; but you must not eat from the tree of the knowing of good and evil, for when you eat from it will you will certainly die."

    (Genesis 2:16-17)

- Adam blamed Eve.

    The man said, "The woman you put here with me-she gave me some fruit from the tree, and I ate it."

    (Genesis 3:12)

- Adam refused to take responsibility.

    Then the Lord God said to the woman, "what is this you have done?" the woman said, "the serpent deceived me, and I ate."

    (Genesis 3:13)

- Therefore, sin and condemnation have been part of the human condition (see Genesis 3:14-19.)

To achieve his goal, satan:

1. Deceived Eve, who then convinced Adam join with her in sinning against God.
2. Since then, mankind has continued to sin against God and passed this decision from one generation to the next.

When our relationship with God is restored:

1. Our broken "selves" are healed through Christ.
2. We hear God's voice and understand His love.
3. We can choose to forgive those whom we have not been able to forgive in the past.
4. We can take responsibility for our lives instead of blaming others, thereby becoming free from the pain caused by our own bitterness.
5. We realize our need for God as we become humble before Him.

6. We recover our authority as the children of God and rejoice in the renewed fellowship with Him.
7. When our relationship with God is restored, the power and blessing of the Holy Spirit become manifest in our lives.

To be restored:

1. We must receive the forgiveness Jesus has for each of us.
    a. Salvation is free as the Lord has already paid the price.
    b. Restoration is something we pursue as we become willing lay down our lives.
2. To experience the power of the Holy Spirit, we must give up the things of this world.
3. We cannot experience healing and restoration just by thinking about it. We must allow the Lord to do the work He desires. We must also continue to study of the Word, stay in prayer, and live a transformed life.
4. We must continue opening ourselves up to God and allow Him to do the ongoing healing work He wants to do.
5. We must choose to continue saying "no" to our old, destructive ways.
6. It is not enough to drive out demons in the name of Jesus. We must also keep watch so that those demons never come back.
7. Many Christians tend to go back to their old ways after getting what they need from God. We must choose not to be one of these people. Those who continue longing for the ways in which God works and have undying passion and commitment to Him are those who whose passion and love for Him continue to grow stronger by the day.

CHAPTER 3

GOD'S VISION FOR ME

"Where there is no revelation, (Vision) the people cast off restraint; But happy is he who keeps the law."

(Proverbs 29:18)

Vision is where God accomplishes His purpose for us by revealing His intentions to believers.

All journeys have their destinations. Christians have God's divine will and purpose for their lives. Mankind tends to view God's will from their own point of view. In order for us to know God and His will more clearly, we need a higher level of revelation.

To miss God's will for our lives is to miss on our true calling. God knew us before we were even conceived in our mother's womb, and His vision supplies reasons and motives, and aligns us with His purpose.

"You did not choose me, but I chose you and appointed you so that you might go and bear fruit – fruit that will last – so that whatever you ask in my name the Father will give you."

(John 15:16)

"For you created my inmost being; you knit me together in my mother's womb. I praise you because I am fearfully and wonderfully made; your works are wonderful. I know that full well. My frame was not hidden from you when I was made in the secret place, when I was woven together in the depths of the earth. Your eyes saw my unformed body; all the days ordained for me were written in your book before one of them came to be."

(Psalms 139:13-16)

> *"Before I formed you in the womb I knew you, before you were born I set you apart; I appointed you as a prophet to the nations."*
>
> (Jeremiah 1:5)

Questions:

What came first, me or my purpose?
Did God discover my purpose after I was created?
Was I created by coincidence or God's mistake?
Was the purpose of my existence there before I was saved or after?

Who I am today is the reason for my existence.

> *"Praise be to the God and Father of our Lord Jesus Christ, who has blessed us in the heavenly realms with every spiritual blessing in Christ. For he chose us in him before the creation of the world to be holy and blameless in his sight. In love."*
>
> (Ephesians 1:3-4)

We were created by our Creator for His intended purpose. God has given us His grace to accomplish the reason why we have been put here. Grace is God's divine ability to do His will. Faith is the ability to believe God for whatever He calls us to. Before the Creation, the Lord had predestined us to do His good works in accordance with His will.

> *"For it is by grace you have been saved, through faith-and this is not from yourselves, it is the gift of God-not by works, so that no one can boast. For we are God's handiwork, created in Christ Jesus to do good works, which God prepared in advance for us to do."*
>
> (Ephesians 2:8-10)

God wants to restore our vision.

Our vision can be restored when we repent and are transformed in the power of the Holy Spirit. God wants each of us to discover our life's vision and purpose and to live accordingly. Only then can we achieve real success.

Successful people:

- Are focused.
- Have clearly defined vision and are moving according to that vision.
- Are trained in all aspects of life to become suitable for their purpose.
- Are determined.
- Are persistent.
- Are those who do not allow obstacles to stop them.

God promises to guide us to the successful completion of our purpose. He has the processes through which He helps us to reach our full potential. All whom God has called must go through this process of preparation.

> *"For the Spirit God gave us does not make us timid, but gives us power, love, and self-discipline. So do not be ashamed of the testimony about our Lord or of me his prisoner. Rather, join with me in suffering for the gospel, by the power of God. He has saved us and called us to a holy life- not because of anything we have done but because of his own purpose and grace. This grace was given us in Christ Jesus before the beginning of time."*
> (2 Timothy 1:7-9)

Those of us who have been saved have the duty to be His witnesses. The Holy Spirit is given to us to accomplish God's will and vision. To be saved is to be called by God, and our lives must be dedicated to carry out His will; we must live as a witness to His healing and salvation for all mankind.

God's vision helps believers discover their purpose in life and becomes their source of joy and hope. Faith with vision grants freedom to do God's will, and it is key to freedom from an oppressed life of bondage. He requires us to have an obedient and humble attitude, as we seek Him above all things.

Vision gives us motivation for submitting to Jesus as Lord and obeying His Word. Vision gives us the will to free ourselves from things of this world. Those who have a vision are more willing to deny themselves and to make sacrifices. Ask yourself this question: Which would have been easier for God, to prepare our purpose or to prepare US for His purpose?

> *"And we know that in all things God works, for the good of those who love him, who have been called according to his purpose."*
>
> (Romans 8:28)

God transforms us to help us accomplish His purpose for us.

Abraham

> *"By faith Abraham, when God tested him, offered Isaac as a sacrifice. He who had embraced the promises was about to sacrifice his one and only son."*
>
> (Hebrews 11:17)

> *"Blessed is the one who perseveres under trial because, having stood the test, that person will receive the crown of life that the Lord has promised to those who love him. When tempted, no one should say, "God is tempting me." For God cannot be tempted by evil, nor does he tempt anyone; but each person is tempted when they are dragged away by their own evil desire and enticed."*
>
> (James 1:12-14)

We must realize that what is within us can defeat us. We have been broken because of our sins, but God desires to make us whole again.

Peter

> *"Simon, Simon, Satan has asked to sift all of you as wheat. But I have prayed for you, Simon, that your faith may not fail. And when you have turned back, strengthen your brothers." But he replied, "Lord, I am ready*

to go with you to prison and to death." Jesus answered, "I tell you Peter, before the rooster crows today, you will deny three times that you know me."
(Luke 22:31-34)

Keep in mind that the way God chooses to change us may include the people around us, such as friends, relationships, spouses, parents, children, employer, employee, and church members.

How do we gain understanding of God's vision?

1. The Lord's vision is always based on the Word of God. This vision gives glory to the Lord, instead of to man.

   Therefore, as it is written: "Let the one who boasts boast in the Lord."
   (1 Corinthians 1:31)

2. God's vision always shows us who we are, including our weaknesses and our shortcomings. When the Lord gives us a vision, our first reaction might be to doubt ourselves. We may say, "But I can't do that!!"

   "I can do everything through him who gives me strength."
   (Philippians 4:13)

   The fact that we cannot do anything apart from God is one of the hardest lessons we learn and one of the easiest lessons to forget. He desires that we remain in Him and bear much fruit.

   "I am the vine; you are the branches. If you remain in me and I in you, you will bear much fruit; apart from me you can do nothing."
   (John 15:5)

3. God's vision demands that we give up things of this world.

   "I tell you, not one of those who were invited will get a taste of my banquet." Large crowds were traveling with Jesus and turning to them he

said: "If anyone comes to me and does not hate father and mother, wife and children, brothers and sisters-yes, even their own life-such a person cannot be my disciple. And whoever does not carry their cross and follow me cannot be my disciple. "Suppose one of you wants to build a tower. Won't you first sit down and estimate the cost to see if you have enough money to complete it? For if you laid the foundation and are not able to finish it, everyone who sees it will ridicule you saying, 'This person began to build and wasn't able to finish' "Or" suppose a king is about to go to war against another king. Won't he first sit down and consider whether he is able with ten thousand men to oppose the one coming against him with twenty thousand? If he is not able, he will send a delegation while the other is still a long way off and will ask for terms of peace. In the same way, those of you who do not give up everything you have cannot be my disciples."

(Luke 14:27-33)

If we cannot sacrifice our ideals or plans for the sake of God's vision, we can never succeed. If we continue to cut corners in serving the Lord, we can never succeed. Unless we are determined to do whatever it takes for the sake of His vision, we cannot demand others to make any commitment to the Lord.

Salvation was given to us without any price. But to achieve God's vision, we must pay the price, and the price we are called to pay is to give up our lives for Him. Jesus sacrificed His life to accomplish the will of God, and He calls us to do the same.

Throughout the Bible, God calls His people to sacrifice, and to sacrifice means to "give up" or to "die to oneself."

4. God's vision may seem impossible to us. However, we must persevere with strong faith, patience, and obedience to God, knowing that He will supply all that we need.

"If you are willing and obedient, you will eat the good things of the land."
(Isaiah 1:19)

"You need to persevere so that when you have done the will of God, you will receive what he has promised."
(Hebrews 10:36)

5. Vision will always be tested, but a true vision from God will always pass the test. The biggest challenge we face is to believe God.

   "In all this you greatly rejoice, though now for a little while you may have had to suffer grief in all kinds of trials. These have come so that the proven genuineness of your faith-of greater worth than gold, which perishes even though refined by fire-may result in praise, glory and honor when Jesus Christ is revealed."

   (1 Peter 1:6-7)

   A good example is found in Genesis 22:1-14, the story of Abraham.

To fulfill the Lord's vision and purpose we must do the following:

1. Have a sincere desire to follow God.

   "The one who sent me is with me; he had not left me alone, for I always do what pleases him."

   (John 8:29)

   "Take delight in the Lord and he will give you the desires of your heart."

   (Psalms 37:4)

   Successful people concentrate all their energy to fulfill their purpose. When you yearn for the Lord in all you do, He will make Himself known to you.

2. Focus on His vision and purpose.

   "Not that I have already obtained all this, or have already arrived at my goal, but I press on to take hold of that for which Christ Jesus took hold of me. Brothers and sisters, I do not consider myself yet to have taken hold of it. But one thing I do; Forgetting what is behind and straining toward what is ahead, I press on toward the goal to win the prize for which God has called me heavenward in Christ Jesus."

   (Philippians 3:12-14)

God calls us to:
- Forget what is behind you, get healed and move on. Forgive and be forgiven from the wounds that others have inflicted on you and your own failures.
- To win the prize for which God has called us we must focus on the vision.

3. Self-training and self-denial. This includes:
   - Meditating on the Word, praying in the Holy Spirit, spending time in worship, building your fellowship with the Lord.
   - Finding your place in the local church and a place to serve.
   - Serving your neighbors and be God's witness.
   - Finding and growing in your God-given gifts.
   - Consistently examining yourself and striving to live in holiness, and free of sin.
   - Training yourself to control your mind, your will, and your emotions.
   - Denying yourself by taking up your cross daily.

4. Must have the determination to follow the vision and never give up.
   Take some time to read Mark 5, the story of a woman who had been "bleeding" for many years.

   Successful people have strong determination and they rarely give up. People who are determined do not give into failures that come their way. If they fail, they get right back up and try again. Success is getting up one more time after you fail.

   "For though the righteous fall seven times, they rise again, but the wicked stumble when calamity strikes."

   (Proverbs 24:16)

   "And but my righteous one will live by faith. And I take no pleasure in the one who shrinks back."

   (Hebrews 10:38)

5. God's vision requires patience.

   "Then the Lord replied: Write down the revelation and make it plain on tablets so that a herald my run with it. For the revelation awaits an

appointed time; it speaks of the end and will not prove false. Though it lingers, wait for it; it will come and not delay."

(Habakkuk 2:2-3)

It is important to clearly write down the vision God gives us so that we fully understand it and patiently wait.

- It helps us bear witness to the Word of God.
- It helps us to pray according to God's leading.
- It presents clarity of purpose in life and helps us to remain focused.
- It helps us to use our resources wisely.
- It guides us to a peaceful and desirable relationship with the Lord, and allows us to be courageous and confident in the fact that the Lord is with us and will continually work in us to do His will.

CHAPTER 4

THE VOICE OF GOD

While many know *about* God, few truly *know* God. God is looking for those who seek his face and have "ears to hear" and a heart to understand what He is saying (see Matthew 13:9-16). The Holy Spirit wants to teach us how to listen to God's voice. God is speaking to us even now. To those who keep their ears open and *really* listen, are those who have fellowship with Him and receive His guidance and comfort.

There are people who recognize God's voice and live according to the Lord's will. There are also many who claim, "God has spoken to me" and speak their minds as if it were God's voice. The truth is that not all who claim to have heard from God truly have heard from Him.

It is unfortunate that there is so much misunderstanding today regarding hearing the voice of God. This is because of a lack of understanding, and very little biblical teaching.

> "As has just been said: "Today, if you hear his voice, do not harden your hearts as you did in the rebellion."
>
> (Hebrews 3:15)

The Apostle Paul forewarned us of many voices in this world and of many who claim to be that of God (see 2 Corinthians 11:13). If you believe all those voices to be that of God you can easily become a victim of satan's delusion. We must also remember that there are voices of the human will, of our ideas and thoughts, of our enemies, and of this world, and we are easily misled by our emotions, and can mistake any of these to be God's voice.

We are prone to make mistakes. Only a fool would claim everything they hear is the voice of God. We are all proud, ambitious, and greedy. We have "stumbling blocks" in our hearts caused by our own sins. All of these make it hard for us to hear God's voice.

Many Christians mistake their own wishes to be the voice of God. People tend to hear what they want to hear. God's voice will be heard by those who give themselves fully to the Lord and humbly seek His face with sincere and pure hearts.

> *"My sheep listen to my voice; I know them, and they follow me."*
> (John 10:27)

> *"The gatekeeper opens the gate for him, and the sheep listen to his voice. He calls his own sheep by name and leads them out. When he has brought out all his own, he goes on ahead of them, and his sheep follow him because they know his voice. But they will never follow a stranger, in fact, they will run away from him because they do not recognize a stranger's voice."*
> (John 10:3-5)

These scriptures tell us that we can hear the voice of God. It also tells us that we will receive His guidance when we hear His voice and follow it. However, the problem is that His sheep are not taught to hear His voice.

If a stranger calls, you would not want to engage in a long conversation with him. Instead, you would try end the conversation as soon as possible. But if a friend calls, you tend to have a longer, more comfortable dialogue.

When it comes to hearing God, there are many times when we do not recognize the source: Is this God? Is it satan? Is it me? There are countless occasions where we do not know how to respond to this voice we hear and find ourselves in confusion.

We are at a loss when we are faced with an issue and we do not hear God's voice. When this happens, we seek help from one person to the next, but their opinions and advice are not always consistent, which puts us in an even bigger bind. It becomes unclear whose voice we are following.

However, to truly hear and know the voice of God, we need to know the Word. The Bible says that faith comes from hearing and hearing comes from the Word of God (see Romans 10:17). We will have faith when we hear His message (voice), and we will obey His direction. We will also be able to confront and hold our own against satan's tactics. Because we clearly know that God is with us, we have the strength to fight spiritual battles.

To hear God's voice is a privilege that born again Christians have. God created us to have an intimate relationship with Him, including hearing Him even as He hears us.

Even now, God is speaking to us. Then why can't we hear Him?

"In them is fulfilled the prophecy of Isaiah: 'You will be ever hearing but never understanding; you will be ever seeing but never perceiving. For this people's heart has become calloused; they hardly hear with their ears, and they have closed their eyes. Otherwise, they might see with their eyes, hear with their ears, understand with their hearts, and turn, and I would heal them."

(Matthew 13:14-15)

If we hear His words, we must also respond appropriately and obey Him.

"This is the verdict: Light has come into the world, but people loved darkness instead of light because their deeds were evil. Everyone who does evil hates the light and will not come into the light for fear that their deeds will be exposed."

(John 3:19-20)

However, we are afraid of our sins being exposed, so we close our hearts in order to hide them. When we do not open our hearts to God, we will eventually become dull of hearing the voice of God.

As has just been said: "Today, if you hear his voice, do not harden your hearts as you did in the rebellion." Who were they who heard and rebelled? Were they not all those Moses led out of Egypt? And with whom was he angry for forty years? Was it not with those who sinned, whose bodies perished in the wilderness? And to whom did God swear that they would never enter his rest if not to those who disobeyed? So, we see that they were not able to enter, because of their unbelief."

(Hebrews 3:15-19)

The Bible also tells that we cannot hear His voice because of our disobedience and our unbelief. To have a hardened heart means to be stubborn and self-centered, and our disobedience is the end result. How does our spirit become hardened? When we merely listen to the words of God, but we choose not to obey.

> *"Others, like seed sown on rocky places, hear the word and at once receive it with joy. But since they have no root, they last only a short time. When trouble or persecution comes because of the world, they quickly fall away."*
> (Mark 4:16-17)

We initially receive His words with joy, but do not follow through with obedience. If the Word cannot find root in our hearts, it cannot transform our lives. If we do not train our ears to hear and recognize His voice, then it will gradually fade and become more and more difficult to understand.

Our disobedience, stubbornness, and unbelief will make our once-tender heart to become hard as a rock. Let's examine how our hearts are hardened by using *cholesterol* in our body as an example.

Consuming greasy food in excess will result in bad cholesterol accumulating in our body, which can be fatal. Spiritually it works the same way. Disobedience and unbelief are like spiritual cholesterol; they will harden our hearts. When we refuse to trust in the Lord and ignore His words of encouragement, spiritual cholesterol will start to accumulate. You may not notice it at first, but eventually you will become completely deaf to His voice. Spiritual deafness is a sure sign of a hard heart, and when we lean on our own wisdom and intelligence, we lose our spiritual sensibility.

An unforgiving attitude and deep-rooted bitterness will also harden our heart. The Bible tells us to be forgiving to one another. While it might not be easy to go and apologize for our wrong doings, or to forgive those who have hurt us, we are commanded to do so. The good news is that forgiveness is one of God's prescriptions for a hard heart.

If we wait for someone else to apologize first instead of taking that first step to forgive, a root of bitterness will take hold in our hearts. Bitterness can grow quickly, bearing its fruit. It can rob us of our joy and can cause more pain for ourselves and others, because it is one of the main devices that satan uses. We can easily become a victim of his continued attacks, and he will eventually trample our faith and make us feel defeated.

How do you know if your heart has been hardened? Ask yourself if any of the following control you: lies, anger, resentment, bitterness and blame, a sense of guilt, anxiety and impatience, fear and terror, jealousy, and envy. Any of these can put you in bondage to the powers of darkness, can cause depression, and may cause you to consider harming yourself or others. Always remember that bitterness of heart makes you unhappy about anything and everything, regardless of how much love and care others show you.

If we are to learn and understand God's plan for us, we must first be able to hear His voice.

Consider the following scriptures:

> *"A person's steps are directed by the Lord. How then can anyone understand their own way?"*
>
> (Proverbs 20:24)

> *"Whoever belongs to God hears what God says. The reason you do not hear is that you do not belong to God."*
>
> (John 8:47)

> *"Everyone on the side of truth listens to me."*
>
> (John 18:37)

What must we do if we want to hear God?

> *"Sow righteousness for yourselves, reap the fruit of unfailing love and break up your unplowed ground; for it is time to seek the Lord, until he comes and showers his righteousness on you."*
>
> (Hosea 10:12)

In the above scripture, God encourages the people of Israel to repent of their wickedness, return to Him, and be transformed. Today, God is telling us the same. To break up your "unplowed ground" means to break up the hardness of your heart. This includes confession of sins and repentance in order to receive God's forgiveness (see 1 John 1:9).

To "shower his righteousness on you" means that God will abundantly give His grace to those who repent. Rain falls from the sky to moisten and to give life to the soil, and to supply the living water to all things living. He is telling us to turn from our old ways of disobedience, wickedness, and unbelief, so that we can be renewed by God.

> *"Even now declares the Lord return to me with all your heart, with fasting weeping and mourning. Rend your heart and not your garments. Return to the Lord your God for he is gracious and compassionate, slow to anger and abounding in love, and he relents from sending calamity."*
>
> (Joel 2:12-13)

What does it mean to rend your heart?

This means to repent of our sins with true sincerity, and with an open and humble heart.

> *"To the angel of the church in Laodicea write: These are the words of the Amen, the faithful and true witness, the ruler of God's creation. I know your deeds, that you are neither cold nor hot. I wish you were either one or the other! So then, because you are lukewarm, and neither cold nor hot, I will spit you out of My mouth."*
>
> (Revelations 3:14-16)

This scripture tells of *Christians* whose faith was halfhearted at best. In my opinion, a believer with halfhearted faith is no different than those with hardened hearts. They may say with their lips, "I love you Lord" and they may know about God, but their hearts are far away from the Lord. The faith of these believers is always unstable. They vow to serve God but have second thoughts the next moment when God asks them to do something they are unwilling to. The above scripture tells us half-hearted Christians will be spit out.

God separates those who have spiritual thirst and want to hear His voice and obey Him from those who do not. And He will pour out His abounding grace in their everyday life. However, He will spit out those who continue to reject and disobey Him. When the time comes, their heart will be hardened, their ties to God will be broken, and God cannot use them.

> *"Here I am! I stand at the door and knock. If anyone hears my voice and opens the door, I will come in and eat with that person, and they with me."*
>
> (Revelation 3:20)

This is a call to every Christian throughout the world.

> *"Those whom I love I rebuke and discipline. So be earnest and repent."*
> (Revelation 3:19)

This is God's command to all Christians. We can deceive man but we cannot deceive God who examines the heart.

> *"If we confess our sins, he is faithful and just and will forgive us our sins and purify us from all unrighteousness."*
> (1 John 1:9)

> *"My sacrifice, O God, is a broken spirit; a broken and contrite heart you, God, will not despise."*
> (Psalms 51:17)

God tells us that He will give renewed and tender spirits to those who repent of their sins and turn from their old ways.

> *"I will sprinkle clean water on you, and you will be clean; I will cleanse you from all your impurities and from all your idols. I will give you a new heart and put a new spirit in you. I will remove from you your heart of stone and give you a heart of flesh. And I will put my Spirit in you and move you to follow my decrees and be careful to keep my laws."*
> (Ezekiel 36:25-27)

To hear God's voice, you must first have a good relationship with God by giving your life to Jesus and by being spiritually born again.

To become born again, you need to:

- Admit you are a sinner and repent of your sins.

> *"For all have sinned and fall short of the glory of God."*
> (Romans 3:23)

> *"If we confess our sins, he is faithful and just and will forgive us our sins and purify us from all unrighteousness."*
>
> (1 John 1:9)

- Believe that Christ died on the cross and that He was resurrected to save us from our sins and to give us eternal life.

> *"For Christ also suffered once for sins, the righteous for the unrighteous, to bring you to God. He was put to death in the body but made alive in the Spirit."*
>
> (1 Peter 3:18)

- Accept through faith that God has given us His son Jesus Christ as a gift.

> *"For God so loved the world that he gave his one and only Son, that whoever believes in him shall not perish but have eternal life."*
>
> (John 3:16)

- Lean on the Lord Jesus Christ entirely and follow Him, obey Him, and serve Him unconditionally (see Matthew 10:37-38; Luke 18:29-30).

> *"Whoever believes in the Son has eternal life, but whoever rejects the Son will not see life, for God's wrath remains on them."*
>
> (John 3:36)

- Declare before others that you belong to Jesus Christ.

> *"Whoever acknowledges me before other, I will also acknowledge before my Father in heaven. But whoever disowns me before others, I will disown before my Father in heaven."*
>
> (Matthew 10:32-33)

> *"Whoever is ashamed of me and my words, the Son of Man will be ashamed of them when he comes in his glory and in the glory of the Father and of the holy angels."*
>
> (Luke 9:26)

- Acknowledge that Jesus Christ not only died on the cross to give us eternal life, but also that He rose again from the dead and His life is in us eternally.

    "And this is the testimony: God has given us eternal life, and this life is in his Son. Whoever has the Son has life; whoever does not have the Son of God does not have life."

    (1 John 5:11-12)

CHAPTER 5

THOSE WHO HEAR GOD'S VOICE

People who heard the voice of God in the Old Testament.

God's voice is not a mystery; He has been speaking since the beginning of time.

1. First, Adam and Eve, heard the voice of God. But their sins denied their access to God and His voice.

   "Then the man and his wife heard of the Lord God as he was walking in the garden in the cool of the day, and they hid from the Lord God among the trees of the garden."

   (Genesis 3:8)

2. Abraham was able to hear God and obey Him, which allowed him to become the Father of our faith.

   "And through your offspring all nations on the earth will be blessed because you have obeyed me."

   (Genesis 22:18)

3. Moses communicated with God as if between two friends.

   Remember the day you stood before the Lord your God at Horeb, when he said to me, "Assemble the people before me to hear my words so that they may learn to revere me as long as they live in the land and may teach them to their children."

   (Deuteronomy 4:10)

However, in Moses' day, the people of Israel actively avoided hearing His voice.

> *"But now, why should we die? This great fire will consume us, and we will die if we hear the voice of the Lord or God any longer. For what mortal has ever heard the voice of the living God speaking out of fire, as we have, and survived? Go near and listen to all that the Lord our God says. Then tell us whatever the Lord our God tells you. We will listen and obey."*
>
> (Deuteronomy 5:25-27)

Just as the Israelites preferred to hear from God through Moses, many Christians today do not want the responsibility of hearing God directly. They want to hear God's messages from their pastors or other servants of God. In the end, teachers, pastors, and other servants of God become "God's voice" to these individuals. However, true believers must be able to hear God for themselves and separate it from what they hear from others.

Because people do not know the Lord's voice, they listen to messages that are pleasing to their ears, something the Bible calls "itching ear doctrine" (see 2 Timothy 4:3-4). Unfortunately, many do not even believe that God still speaks to us today. They believe that God now only speaks through the Bible. Of course, what God tells us today must not contradict the truth found in the scriptures in any way.

We know that God spoke to man in the days of the Old Testament. But what about in the New Testament days?

God spoke to Saul who later became Paul on his way to Damascus.

> *As he neared Damascus on his journey, suddenly a light from heaven flashed around him. He fell to the ground and heard a voice say to him, "Saul, Saul, why do you persecute me?"*
>
> (Acts 9:3-4)

Peter heard God's voice in his prayer.

> *Then I heard a voice telling me, 'Get up, Peter. Kill and eat.' "I replied, 'Surely not, Lord! Nothing impure or unclean has ever entered my mouth.'" The voice spoke from heaven a second time, 'Do not call anything impure*

that God has made clean.' This happened three times, and then it was pulled up to heaven again."

(Acts 11:7-10)

Five Requirements to Hearing God's Voice.

Humility

Humility is one of the most important requirements in being able to hear God. When we humble ourselves before the Lord, we take a step towards a higher spiritual level. The Bible clearly indicates that there will be no progress without humbleness as we seek God's guidance. God is against arrogance: *"But he gives us more grace. That is why Scripture says: 'God opposes the proud but shows favor to the humble'"* (James 4:6). Those who are proud do not feel the need to put in the time to seek the Lord's face. They make decisions relying on their own judgment and intellect. However, life independent from God is arrogant and foolish in His eyes.

> *"God looks down from heaven on all mankind to see if there are any who understand, any who seek God."*
>
> (Psalms 53:2)

It is the work of the Holy Spirit in our lives that causes us to seek God. We generally seek God's counsel for important matters, but not for those we consider trivial; we feel we can't or should not bother God. However, there is real danger in making decisions while relying on our own judgment without seeking God's counsel. Jesus never relied on His assumptions or judgment; He sought God's will in all things, big or small.

Faith

Faith is the second requirement in being able to hear God. We must believe that our God is a living God.

> *"And without faith it is impossible to please God, because anyone who comes to him must believe that he exists and that he rewards those who earnestly seek him."*
>
> (Hebrews 11:6)

Our living God is all knowing; He knows where we are, what we do, and why we do it.

- Only our God of perfect justice can judge what is right and just, for our lives and those whom our decisions will influence.
- Our Holy God never told us to act on things that are against His character or that are against principles found in the Bible. The only thing He wants us to do is obey His words and to follow His will through faith.
- When we obey God, we get to know His ways and become stronger in faith.

> *"I will instruct you and teach you in the way you should go; I will counsel you with my loving eye on you."*
>
> (Psalms 32:8)

> *"For this God is our God for ever and ever, he will be our guide even to the end."*
>
> (Psalms 48:14)

> *Whether you turn to the right or to the left, your ears will hear a voice behind you, saying, "This is the way, walk in it."*
>
> (Isaiah 30:21)

> *"This is what the Lord says – your redeemer, the Holy One of Israel: I am the Lord your God, who teaches you what is best for you, who directs you in the way you should go."*
>
> (Isaiah 48:17)

Pure Heart

The third requirement is a pure heart.

> *"Blessed are the pure in heart, for they will see God."*
>
> (Matthew 5:8)

From time to time, we must come to the Lord and give Him the time He requires to help us see our sins.

"If I had cherished sin in my heart, the Lord would not have listened."
(Psalms 66:18)

To keep our hearts pure, we must examine ourselves for any unconfessed sin. At times, God's silence may be because of the inequities we have been harboring. For example, when the chief priests and teachers of the law were not being truthful in their answers, Jesus refused to speak to them (see Luke 20:1-8).

When we open our hearts and seek His face, God helps us see that we have either a wrong impression or mindset about a situation, and makes us aware of the times we were disobedient to Him. When we sincerely repent—repentance means to "turn away" or "go another way"—God will be faithful to guide us to the right path.

"I walk in the way of righteousness, along the paths of justice."
(Proverbs 8:20)

Renouncing your will

The fourth requirement is to renounce your will. Your will is what you use to determine the direction you take. Your commitment to follow God's will is necessary if you want to receive His guidance. If you sincerely desire to walk with God and give yourself wholly to Him, He will guide you in His own way.

Keep in mind that:

- Following your own voice or that of satan is only for your own selfish reasons.
- If you acknowledge your mistakes and turn from them, and choose to live according to His ways, God's plan for your future will more than make up for any of your past failures.

Wait before Him

The fifth requirement to wait before Him is the most difficult. We must give Him time for Him to speak to us.

- When we hear God, the focus of our attention must be on Him, not on us.
- Even if what He wants does not agree with what we want, we must choose to unconditionally obey and follow Him (see Luke 22:42).

> *"But my people would not listen to me; Israel would not submit to me. So, I gave them over to their stubborn hearts to follow their own devices. If my people would only listen to me, if Israel would only follow my ways."*
>
> (Psalms 81:11-13)

A good example is Peter. He was never hesitant in voicing his opinions, which he boldly stated at Mount Tabor (the Mount of Transfiguration, see Matthew 16:22-28).

- God spoke to Peter directly about Jesus.

> *"This is my son, whom I love; with him I am well pleased. Listen to him!"*
>
> (Matthew 17:5)

We must hear the voice of God, who called us when we became born again and is calling us now. Like Peter, God wants us to completely change our ways so that God's will would be done through our lives. When we learn to wait for God and let ourselves depend solely on the Holy Spirit, God will turn our biggest weaknesses into our greatest strengths.

Knowing where a voice is coming from

We must be aware of and to distinguish between the four sources that bring about an impression or feelings within us.

My own ideas

- Refers to those based on human logic.
- Human logic is the way things should be, in our opinion.
- The Bible clearly tells us how foolish it is to depend on our own reason and intelligence.

> *"Those who trust in themselves are fools."*
>
> (Proverbs 28:26)

Instead, God calls us to …

"Trust in the Lord with all your heart and lean not on your own understanding."

(Proverbs 3:5)

And we are to …

"We demolish arguments and every pretension that sets itself up against the knowledge of God, and we take captive every thought to make it obedient to Christ."

(2 Corinthians 10:5)

"For my thoughts are not your thoughts, neither are your ways my ways, declares the Lord."

(Isaiah 55:8)

Impressions or Emotions

These may come from our own needs, wants, and desires, which can be overwhelming at times. We must be completely honest about how we feel or think regarding a situation, and make the same confession that Jesus made in the garden: "Yet not my will but yours be done" (Luke 22:42). We must not allow our desires to determine our will.

"In the same way, count yourselves dead to sin but alive to God in Christ Jesus."

(Romans 6:11)

Satan's voice:

- Leads us into deception by twisting or quoting Scripture out of context.
- Makes us uneasy and impatient.
- Drives us to a crisis so that we act quickly without waiting for God's time.
- His desire is to destroy our life, steal our blessings and leads us to fall.

> *"The thief comes only to steal and kill and destroy; I have come that they may have life, and have it to the full."*
>
> (John 10:10)

God's voice:

- Quiet and consistent.
- Heard mainly as a soft and delicate voice (see 1 Kings 19:11-13).
- The Peace of God that transcends all understanding will guide our hearts and minds. If there is no peace it is not God.

> *"And the peace of God which transcends all understanding, will guard your hearts and your minds in Christ Jesus."*
>
> (Philippians 4:7)

> *"Now may the Lord of peace himself give you peace at all times and in every way. The Lord be with all of you."*
>
> (2 Thessalonians 3:16)

We must always test to see where certain impressions/feelings are coming from.

God speaks through:

1. The Bible.
2. What we see in the natural (Romans 1:20).
3. Visions, dreams, angels (Exodus 31:18, Daniel 5:24, John 8:5-9).
4. Creation which shows the glory of God (Psalms 19:1-4, Romans 1:20).
5. Pillars of fire and cloud, consuming fire (Exodus 24:17), and supernatural signs (Judges 6:21, 36-40; Isaiah 38; 1 Samuel 14:10).
6. What we hear through trusted sources.
7. Voices we hear in our hearts (John 10:27, 10:3-4).
8. Music and poetry, testimonies, voices we hear with our ears (Acts 9:4-6).
9. People (1 Samuel 12:1-12, 1 Kings 13).
10. The impression in our spirit, strong conviction, and peace (Romans 8:6).
11. The Holy Spirit's commands (Isaiah 55:8-9).
12. Strong feelings or impressions.

How do we confirm that God is speaking to us?

- God's voice always brings us closer to Jesus and humbles us. In Revelation 1:17, John said the following after hearing God's voice: "When I saw him, I fell at his feet as though dead."
- The presence of God will always accompany His voice, and our life will be filled with joy through His presence and glory.
- The Lord's voice brings biblical conviction.
- The Holy Spirit gives us confirmation about the Scripture.
- God's voice always agrees with the scriptures.
- God brings a truly divine authority in whatever He says. The Word of God is not secret revelations; it can be openly shared and confirmed with others.

Most important, we must know the foundational doctrines of our Christian faith that we may discern any error.

Knowing the Word of God on continually deeper levels allows you to hear God's voice more clearly. Our mind works like a computer; what you input determines the output. Negative input leads to negative output; positive input leads to positive output.

By reading and studying the Word, you are absorbing it into your spirit. When the Word is in you, you hear God's voice more clearly. If you do not know the Word of God, it is much harder to discern God's voice.

God created us in his image because He wanted to have a relationship with us. He wants to have a close, intimate relationship like that between parents and their children. If our relationship with God resembles that of a master and a servant, we cannot expect to draw closer to God and feel fulfillment in our relationship with Him. God calls us His friends, not slaves. We are His sons and daughters, a part of His family, and not hired workers.

> *"Enoch walked faithfully with God; then he was no more, because God took him away."*
>
> (Genesis 5:14)

Enoch's relationship with God is an example of how intimate the Christian life should be.

CHAPTER 6

HEALING FOR THE ROOT OF BITTERNESS

"I am the vine; you are the branches. If you remain in me and I in you, you will bear much fruit; apart from me you can do nothing. If you do not remain in me, you are like a branch that is thrown away and withers; such branches are picked up, thrown into the fire and burned. If you remain in me and my words remain in you, ask whatever you wish, and it will be done for you. This is to my Father's glory, that you bear much fruit, showing yourselves to be my disciples."

(John 15:5-8)

"You did not choose me, but I chose you and appointed you so that you might go and bear fruit-fruit that will last-and so that whatever you ask in my name the Father will give you."

(John 15:16)

If our life fails to bear good fruits in the Kingdom of God, can we honestly say that we are living a life of a true Christian? The life of a believer must have the power of Christ's life in order to have something to offer to this world. All things living have in their nature the ability to bear fruit.

The Christian life that bears fruit can be defined by the answers to the following questions:

- How many have received salvation through our witness and because of our lifestyle?
- How many have received the gift of the Holy Spirit through us?
- Is God's glory revealed in us?

> *"But the fruit of the Spirit is love, joy, peace, forbearance, kindness, goodness, faithfulness, gentleness, and self-control. Against such things there is no law."*
>
> (Galatians 5:22-23)

If we cannot produce these good fruits, there is a problem within us. It is harder to follow His will or act within His plan for us, and we are hindered from completing the mission to which we have been called.

> *The people of the city said to Elisha, "Look, or Lord, this town is well situated, as you can see, but water is bad, and the land is unproductive."*
>
> (2 Kings 2:19)

Our reactions to our surroundings depend on what is inside of us. If there is "filthy water" flowing through us, our responses will not be right; we will display the fruit of the flesh.

> *"The acts of the flesh are obvious: sexual immorality, impurity, and debauchery; idolatry and witchcraft; hatred, discord, jealously, fits of rage, selfish ambition, dissensions, factions and envy; drunkenness, orgies, and the like. I warn you, as I did before, that those who live like this will not inherit the kingdom of God."*
>
> (Galatians 5:19-21)

Whether serious or minor, we will continue running into problems. What we focus on determines whether or not we can improve the character and quality of our lives through these various events, rather than the events themselves determining our character. We can either please God or disappoint Him through our responses and attitudes towards our circumstances. To cause God concern is no different than to interfere with His plans for our lives.

"Bitter water" flowing through us manifests itself through an unforgiving heart, disobedience, pride, resentment, doubt, bigotry, wickedness, and more. These unwanted traits are often caused by the wounds of our past. No one is exempt from all rejections, big or small. Rejection can happen to anyone, anytime. Where we have deep rooted wounds, satan takes advantage and causes feelings of shame, guilt, judgment, etc., to take control of our thoughts. The root of rejection may have come from others or circumstances beyond our control, but in the end, it results in rejecting ourselves and others. When we have been rejected, we reject others as a form of self-defense.

Some people openly recall those painful memories of rejection, while the others completely ignore them and do their best to erase these memories completely from their mind. However, the subconscious mind does not forget what has happened.

What can you do to stop this "bitter water" from flowing and ruining your life?

To have your spiritual wounds healed, you first must recognize the source of these wounds.

> *"Search me God and know my heart; test me and know my anxious thoughts. See if there is any offensive way in me and lead me in the way everlasting."*
>
> (Psalms 139:23-24)

The first step towards healing is to open your heart so that the Holy Spirit can reveal what is inside your soul that is causing you pain. When the Spirit shows you the cause of your problems, you must acknowledge and confront them, and obey and follow the Holy Spirit's leading to your path of healing. Then He can heal your hurts so they no longer affect your life. When He does this, you can experience the true freedom God has for you.

This freedom will become stronger by the day, bringing healing in greater depths. Just as you get better and are finally able to beat an illness when you continue to follow your doctor's advice, your life will be filled with joy, peace, and righteousness as you follow God's path of healing. This is true freedom.

> *"For I know the plans I have for you, declares the Lord, plans to prosper you and not to harm you, plans to give you hope and a future."*
>
> (Jeremiah 29:11)

If you do not properly handle the negative feelings that can sometimes consume you, you may rebel against God and others through disobedience, even after you discover your bitter roots. The wound will become deeper and wider, and the problem will continue to snowball until you address the root cause. If you don't, that "filthy, bitter water" will lead to your destruction, just like a poison.

> *"Bring me a new bowl," he said, "and put salt in it." So, they brought it to him. Then he went out to the spring and threw the salt into it, saying, "This is what the Lord says: 'I have healed this water. Never again will it cause death or make the land unproductive."*
>
> (2 Kings 2:20-21)

This verse speaks about one of God's promises of healing.

Salt has a special meaning in the Bible. The Lord told us we are the salt of this world (Matthew 5:13). A Holy God cannot reside in an impure temple; therefore, God makes us "salty" with salt so that the character of Christ forms within us. This is the power of the salt of the Word that cleanses us and purifies us. (Salt purifies preserves, heals, and adds taste. It also cleanses, causes thirst, and melts ice.)

The spiritual equivalent of salt is humbleness and self-denial. True healing is only possible when we humbly come before the Lord. Without humility, we can never have sincere longing for the Lord. God wants us to come before Him with humble hearts so we can enjoy all the blessings He has prepared for us.

1. We must all be salted with fire. This will purify us and help us through all trials and hardships.

   > *"Everyone will be salted with fire. Salt is good, but if it loses its saltiness, how can you make it salty again? Have salt among yourselves and be a peace with each other."*
   >
   > (Mark 9:49-50)

"Salt with fire" that God uses to cleanse us is the distress, pain, and agony we experience in our relationships until we are healed.

Humility leads us to be at peace with everyone, and without it we lose the peace God gives us. We cannot coexist with others, nor can we reach the spiritual maturity that is essential in a Christian life.

2. Just as salt adds taste to food, it enriches our spiritual life. We must be humble if we are to retain our taste, get along with others, and become useful to God.

> *"You are the salt of the earth. But if the salt loses its saltiness, how can it be made salty again? It is no longer good for anything, except to be thrown out and trampled underfoot."*
>
> (Matthew 5:13)

3. Salt makes us thirsty.

   > *"Blessed are those who hunger and thirst for righteousness, for they will be filled."*
   >
   > (Matthew 5:6)

   God wants us to hunger and thirst for His righteousness. Humility will enable us to have the passion to know and serve God better, and to have a sincere and strong desire to live for His purpose.

   > *"On the last and greatest day of the festival, Jesus stood and said in a loud voice, "Let anyone who is thirsty come to me and drink."*
   >
   > (John 7:37)

   We absolutely and positively need the living water that comes from the Lord. The living water is accessible only through worshiping and spending time with God, and through having a healthy relationship with others. The Lord is not just our Savior and Redeemer, but also the Lord and the Master of our lives.

   We must come before the Lord and confess, "Lord, I do not have the strength to control this bitterness in me; I humbly give them up for you." By doing so, we can finally rid ourselves of this filthy polluted water that taints our spirit.

4. As salt melts ice, our hardened spirit is melted by humility. God wants to soften our hardened heart, which is filled with stubbornness, narrow mindedness, and wicked and revengeful thoughts.

   God promised a renewed spirit and soul, so we can be healed of the hardness of our hearts.

   > *"Sow righteousness for yourselves, reap the fruit of unfailing love, and break up your unplowed ground; for it is time to seek the Lord, until he comes and showers his righteousness on you."*
   >
   > (Hosea 10:12)

We must humbly come before the Lord and confess, "Lord, you are right, and I have been wrong." It's never enough to think that we are right according to our own mindset. We must acknowledge that only God can tell us what is right. When we do that, God will soften our heart.

> *"Even now," declares the Lord, "return to me with all your heart, with fasting and weeping and mourning." Rend your heart and not your garments. Return to the Lord your God, for he is gracious and compassionate, slow to anger and abounding in love, and he relents from sending calamity."*
>
> (Joel 2:12-13)

When we rend our hardened heart of disobedience, God promises His faithfulness, His mercy, and His abounding love. He will give us peace.

5. Salt heals a wound (cleanses it). When we become humble, our spiritual wounds will be healed.

> *"The Spirit of the Sovereign Lord is on me, because the Lord has anointed me to proclaim good news to the poor. He has sent me to bind up the brokenhearted, to proclaim freedom for the captives and release from darkness for the prisoners to proclaim the year of the Lord's favor and the day of vengeance of our God to comfort all who mourn and provide for those who grieve in Zion—to bestow on them a crown of beauty instead of ashes, the oil of joy instead of mourning, and a garment of praise instead of a spirit of despair. They will be called oaks of righteousness, a planting of the Lord for the display of his splendor."*
>
> (Isaiah 61:1-3)

Jesus came:

- To give us hope.
- To embrace our wounded spirit.
- To show God's work in our life.
- To heal us.
- To free us from being a prisoner of sins.

"The Lord is close to the brokenhearted and saves those who are crushed in spirit."

(Psalms 34:18)

In the book of Isaiah, the Lord promises a crown of beauty instead of ashes, the oil of joy instead of mourning, and a garment of praise instead of a spirit of despair, to be called oaks of righteousness (Isaiah 61:1-3). Oak is a strong tree. God created oak trees to illustrate His reach throughout the universe. Like these strong oak trees, God wants each of us to see ourselves as special in His eyes.

6. Salt preserves. God promises to protect us regardless of what we run into in this world.

God has said, "Never will I leave you; never will I forsake you."

(Hebrews 13:5)

"But now, this is what the Lord says—he who created you, Jacob, he who formed you, Israel: "Do not fear, for I have redeemed you; I have summoned you by name; you are mine. When you pass through the waters, I will be with you; and when you pass through the rivers, they will not sweep over you. When you walk through the fire, you will not be burned; the flames will not set you ablaze. For I am the Lord your God, the Holy One of Israel, your Savior; I give Egypt for your ransom. Cush and Seba in your stead."

(Isaiah 43:1-3)

God wants to create His likeness in us, He wants us to be like Him in all we do. God wants to change us from glory to glory. He created us to be just like Him. However, unless we allow God to work within us, we can never know or understand His will.

We must ask the Holy Spirit to change our hearts. When the Spirit of the Lord is upon us, we will have the hope necessary for this change, for this transformation. He transforms us and uses us for His glory. He causes us to say from the bottom of our hearts, "Abba Father, do your will!"

In 1 Peter 5, God says He will lift us up high and make us strong, firm, and steadfast when we become humble in the hands of the Lord. God wants us to heal our hardened soul, we can rid ourselves of pride and bitterness. We must acknowledge and accept that God is right, and we are wrong.

> *"Yet when they were ill, I put on sackcloth and humbled myself with fasting. When my prayers returned to me unanswered."*
>
> (Psalms 35:13)

When we fast and come before the Lord with a humble heart, and when we expose our hardened soul to God, He is faithful to pour out His love, mercy, grace, and compassion. He will forgive our sins and gives us new strength like an eagle (Isaiah 40:31).

Fasting is about self-denial. Self-denial and humbleness go hand in hand.

Here's a good example.

When we make pickles of any kind, we cut vegetables and put them in the salt water to get the taste just right. Just as vegetables become mellow with salt, we must also mellow with humbleness and continue to empty out the "trash" inside of us, so that God can turn us into the design He had in mind when He first created us.

In the following scripture, we see and read of the mission Jesus has for all of us. He died every day and ultimately took up a cross for us. If we are to follow Him as His disciple, we must also die like He did and take up the cross.

> *"Then he said to them all: "Whoever wants to be my disciple must deny themselves and take up their cross daily and follow me."*
>
> (Luke 9:23)

Paul continues this thought.

> *"I have been crucified with Christ and I no longer live, but Christ lives in me. The life I now live in the body, I live by faith in the Son of God, who loved me and gave himself for me."*
>
> (Galatians 2:20)

Death of our pride and self-righteousness

Death of our pride causes us to be joyful in heart despite being forgotten, ignored, or insulted. We consider suffering for Christ as part of our walk with Him.

You know that pride is dead when:

- You can love and persevere.
- You can withstand chaos, disorder, and torment.
- You can confront spiritual apathy, wastefulness, foolishness, and inconsistencies.
- You can be as patient as Jesus.
- You are content with your current situations.
- There is divine intervention based on God's will.
- You do not show yourself off in conversations.
- You can accept advice from your subordinates.
- You no longer have the wickedness or resentment in your heart.

It is not an easy task to kill your pride, but it must be done. Pride is like poison. Pride will interfere with your walk with God. Pride knows nothing but self. Pride says, "My desires, my ideas, my loneliness, my fatigue, injustices done to me." It is always about *me*.

Pride dies only through humility. When you do not surrender to God and His will, it proves that you still have "bitter water" flowing out of your open wounds.

When you cry for change, God who is faithful will free you. When you let everything go, God will re-create you in His image. If you are not interested in denying your pride, don't ask God to use you; He needs to heal you before He can use you.

What if you don't deal with your pride? Bitterness will continue flow, which will keep you distant from God. Pride will hinder your ability to read the Word and pray. It will pollute your soul. It will cause you to be lazy in your relationship with God and with your neighbors. Eventually, pride can cause you to lose interest in the Kingdom of God, and may permanently isolate you from the Body of Christ, and your local church.

The Word says that many have been called, but only few were chosen (see Matthew 22:14). Who is willing to give themselves up for God? Death of your pride means to love your neighbor like yourself. Death to your pride means you accept those who have hurt you. The dead do not move, the dead do not feel any pain. No matter how much you are ignored or forgotten, you can treat others with mercy and compassion. Insult and misunderstanding no longer torment you.

As Elisha eliminated the source of death by putting salt in his bowl of water, we allow the Holy Spirit to "salt" us with fire, the salt of humbleness that kills pride in order to eliminate the root of bitterness in your heart.

Now is the time to reexamine yourself. Get rid of that filthy water flowing through you, which is getting in your way of expanding God's Kingdom, and stopping you from bearing the good fruit of the Holy Spirit.

> *"Search me, God and know my heart; test me and know my anxious thoughts. See if there is any offensive way in me, and lead me in the way everlasting."*
>
> (Psalms 139:23-24)

CHAPTER 7

HEALING THE WOUNDED SOUL

The area that requires the most attention in a man in his soul. Man's illnesses and death are caused by spiritual wounds. Our spiritual wounds are caused by the wrongs that others have done to us, and through our own shortcomings. How we respond to those wrongs also causes these emotional wounds. People hurt one another intentionally or unintentionally.

Man cannot free himself from the shackles and yokes that bind. But the Bible shows us that fasting can help us be free of these evil spirits that oppress us.

> *"Is not this kind of fasting I have chosen: to lose the chains of injustice and untie the cords of the yoke, to set the oppressed free and break every yoke?"*
>
> (Isaiah 58:6)

Blessings that fasting prayer bring us include:

- Leading us to a place where God can get involved.
- Healing our spirit.
- Freeing us from satan.
- Freeing us from all negative influence caused by pain of our past and emotional wounds.
- Breaking the chains of injustice and untie the cords of the yoke, which was put on us because of satan's relentless attacks.

Satan's shackles refer to deeply rooted emotional wounds caused by hurts to our emotions through people or circumstances. Emotional wounds impact us by creating the roots of negativity deep into our soul, which leads to oppression and anxiety, causes various mental disorders, and interferes with our spiritual growth.

We will never experience true joy and freedom in Christ without the healing of our wounded souls.

> *"See to it that no one falls short of the grace of God and that no bitter root grows up to cause trouble and defile many."*
>
> (Hebrews 12:15)

More problems arise if emotional wounds are not healed.

- Emotional wounds are like physical wounds; satan's pressure will aggravate them and we will feel the pain of them every time they are touched.
- Emotional wounds are the open door through which satan can cause havoc in our lives. These openings will become wider and wider, which become the pathway for satan to infiltrate our lives.

Satan accesses our soul through our emotional wounds. They are his opportunity to cause us grief and sorrow. Emotional wounds weaken our will power and hinder us from serving God, and can ultimately destroy us. They will not get better with time, rather a wider variety of emotional side effects will continue to impact our lives.

God's will is to have the human spirit under the control of the Holy Spirit, so that we become Christ-like, and the character of Christ is shown to the world through us. This happens as we get the healing we need from our emotional wounds.

God wants us to be free from our past and to look to the future with hope and joy. He wants us to have the freedom to enjoy life with Him now and in the future. God wants us to be healed emotionally, so we can discover who we really are. He wants us to love ourselves, our family and others. He also wants us to have healthy emotions. In our new found freedom, He wants us to know that He works to make things better in all that He does, and that same freedom will help us reach our fullest potential in Christ. Therefore, we must first allow the Holy Spirit to heal us of deep-seated wounds hidden in the darkest places of our soul.

> *"May God himself, the God of peace, sanctify you through and through. May your whole spirit, soul and body be kept blameless at the coming of our Lord Jesus Christ. The one who calls you is faithful, and he will do it."*
>
> (1 Thessalonians 5:23-24)

The will of God is for our spirit, soul, and body to be fully restored to His likeness.

Consider that grownups still have an inner child within them. This inner child might live with anxiety and fear, due to emotional trauma such as being rejected. God's will is for the inner child to be healed from their insecurity and fears.

Most emotional wounds are caused by rejection.

The feeling of rejection manifests itself in two ways:

- We reject and hate ourselves because of our own experience of being rejected and the hurt we felt.
- We reject others in fear of being rejected again.

Satan takes advantage of our negative reactions received from people or our environment. Satan pays close attention to how we respond when others hurt us or when we face difficult issues.

Feelings of rejection are the cause of almost all of our emotional issues, which then become an obstacle to our spiritual growth, while inviting satan's oppression.

Symptoms and causes of rejection

Symptoms

- Extremely vulnerable emotionally and overly sensitive.
- Angry, critical, judgmental attitude.
- Avoids human relationships and distrusting of others.
- Captivated by fear of being hurt.
- Isolated, self-centered, and selfish.
- Afraid of people.
- Extreme in doctrines and behavior, which may lead to deception.
- Forms mystical, unrealistic, religious actions and thoughts.
- Does whatever it takes to be recognized by others.
- Feels worthless and insecure.
- Tend to self-deprecate, and have a distorted self-image; suffers from an inferiority complex.
- Addiction to alcohol, drugs, rock music, and movies.

- Become a workaholic to escape from reality.
- Panic stricken always thinking something will go wrong.
- Feels like being chased, something going terribly wrong.
- Suffers from inferiority complex, self-hatred, and self-abuse.
- Pessimistic attitude.
- Perfectionist and legalist.
- Have excessive and unrealistic expectation for people. They try hard to be recognized by the people around them through their appearance, positions, or religious performance.

Causes

Feelings of rejection may begin in infancy and evolve through our childhood experiences growing up. The first cause may be from our family. Parents' words, whether negative or positive, have an impact on the formation of a child's self-image.

When the parents do not truly love each other, or a baby is born out of purely sexual desires, or if parents have regrets or shame over having the baby, that child will feel abandoned and rejected. Rejection can also happen when the:

- Father passes away before the child is born.
- Father was absent at birth, for business or other reasons.
- Mother considered abortion during pregnancy.
- Mother was the focus of hurtful arguments or experienced physical abuse during pregnancy.
- Pregnancy was premarital.
- Child was sent to orphanage or adopted immediately after birth.
- Mother was under severe emotional distress during pregnancy.

If the baby was born without true love and was not adequately protected or provided for, there is an open door for oppression by the devil (see Genesis 4:7).

God's will towards family is a place where:

- Love is given and shared.
- A child is accepted and recognized to reach emotional maturity.
- A child learns moral values through his/her parental relationship.
- A child forms his/her self-image and acquires emotional stability.

Unfortunately, parents hurt their children with their words.

- "You are horrible."
- "What can you do right?"
- "Why can't you be like other children? Why can't you be the whole like your brother/sister?"
- "You idiot! What do you think people will say?"
- "You are fat, you are ugly, and you are too skinny!"

> *"The tongue has the power of life and death, and those who love it will eat its fruit."*
>
> (Proverbs 18:21)

Children can be emotionally hurt listening to their parents' conversation with others.

- "I had to marry him; he got me pregnant."
- "*We* weren't even thinking of having a child; he was a mistake."
- "I wanted a daughter (a son), but …"
- "He is so slow to get anything done."
- "He has no future."
- "He is just like his dad, and I hate it."

Words such as these will wound a child's spirit. They can have a direct negative influence on each child by painting distorted self-images on the canvas of their soul.

Parents' actions can emotionally hurt their children.

Parents' divorce or physical and/or sexual abuse can be fatal to children.

Children tend to blame themselves rather than blaming their parents for how they feel. Children do not know why parents speak or behave in negative ways towards them. They don't understand why their parents don't spend time with them, or why they don't say they are loved, or hug or comfort them. Therefore, when these same children grow up and get married, and have children of their own, they unintentionally transfer their emotional baggage to their children.

A parents' lack of affection and/or failure to express their love towards their children can result in one or more of the children becoming rebellious, ashamed, jealous, violent, greedy, disobedient, frustrated, oversensitive, and distrusting of himself, others, and God. As children, they tend to become spiritually and morally lazy. They might stray from God's morality and ethics and live a degenerated lifestyle. They can suffer from chronic depression and do not know how to love or to be loved. As adults, they do not know how to raise their own children with the Word and love of God. As well, it is more likely that they will have difficulty in relationships, experience difficulties in society, or have premarital/extramarital affairs. As adults, they tend to be mentally weak, lack willpower, and can easily give themselves over to hurtful situations. They experience emotional poverty, can become rebellious and violent, and may suffer from fear of rejection leading to hurtful relationships, divorce, and more.

Twelve steps to freedom

Step 1: Open your heart before the Lord and come before Him.

> *"Search me, God, and know my heart; test me and know my anxious thoughts. See if there is any offensive way in me and lead me in the way everlasting."*
>
> (Psalms 139:23-24)

> *"Surely God is my help; the Lord is the one who sustains me."*
>
> (Psalm 54:4)

Step 2: Find the cause.
The cause of our problems is the attacks of satan and our responses. The cause of our pain is not God, our parents, our siblings, people, or our environment. Our pain is caused by the fiery darts satan sends into our minds.

> *"Above all, take the shield of faith, wherewith ye shall be able to quench all the fiery darts of the wicked."*
>
> (Ephesians 6:16)

Step 3: Find the wounds through prayer.
Wounds inflicted in our soul lead to a distorted belief system and self-image. Therefore, we must realize our wounds are caused by satan's lies, then work with the Holy Spirit to bring the healing we need.

> *"Then you will know the truth, and the truth will set you free."*
>
> (John 8:32)

Step 4: Repent of wrong responses.
We must take full responsibility for our misguided reactions, including criticizing others to justify ourselves, then repent of our attitudes and actions. Negative emotions such as anger and resentment, bitterness and displeasure, criticism and judgment can quickly turn into an opportunity for satan.

Repentance destroys satan's foundation and becomes the channel through which we can accept the grace of God.

> *"In the past God overlooked such ignorance, but now he commands all people everywhere to repent."*
>
> (Acts 17:30)

Step 5: Stop criticizing and judging others by forgiving them.
We must stop criticizing and judging those who have caused us pain and forgive them. This will allow us to be free from the roots of bitterness within us. If we are willing to forgive, God will pour out His grace upon us and help us forgive those who we never thought we could forgive.

> *"Be kind and compassionate to one another, forgiving each other, just as in Christ God forgave you."*
>
> (Ephesians 4:32)

Step 6: Confront all falsehood satan has planted within us in the name of Christ Jesus by using God's authority and power. Repent of the sins of our parents and sever the chain of condemnation.
After eliminating the grounds for satan's oppression through repentance and forgiveness, close all doors through which satan can enter with the blood of Jesus Christ.

> *"Submit yourselves, then, to God. Resist the devil, and he will flee from you."*
>
> (James 4:7)

> *Christ redeemed us from the curse of the law by becoming a curse for us, for it is written "Cursed is everyone who is hung on a pole."*
>
> (Galatians 3:13)

Step 7: Forgive yourself of past mistakes. Self-forgiveness is key to God's healing and letting go of your past.
When you feel the urge to go back to your past, praise the Lord and confess your healing victory through proclaiming the Word of God.

> *"Be strong and very courageous. Be careful to obey all the law my servant Moses gave you; do not turn from it to the right or to the left, that you may be successful wherever you go."*
>
> (Joshua 1:7)

> *"Do not conform to the pattern of this world but be transformed by the renewing of your mind."*
>
> (Romans 12:2)

Continue to move towards being filled with the Holy Spirit. Freedom is gained only through action.

Don't give satan an open door by falling into the trap of self-pity, but always protect yourself. Find your place in Jesus Christ by obeying God and protecting your mind.

Step 8: Reconcile
If possible, find ways to mend all broken relationships with your friends and family. The Holy Spirit will guide you regarding the appropriate time and place.

Reconciliation is God's will, but you must wait until the Holy Spirit prepares you and your the other person. Wait for God's time, humbly request God's wisdom, and seek advice from those who can help you.

> *"All this is from God, who reconciled us to himself through Christ and gave us the ministry of reconciliation: that God was reconciling the world to himself in Christ, not counting people's sins against them. And he has, committed to us the message of reconciliation."*
>
> (2 Corinthians 5:18-19)

Step 9: Accepting God's unconditional love is foundational to becoming free from fear of rejection.
True love, peace, and security are found within the love of God. God's love is never failing, is never ending, and is everlasting.

"But God demonstrates his own love for us in this: While we were still sinners, Christ died for us."

(Romans 5:8)

"He who did not spare his own Son, but gave him up for us all-how will he not also, along with him, graciously give us all things?"

(Romans 8:32)

Step 10: Know that we are God's children.
When we know that are the beloved sons and daughters of God, we will no longer fear any and all forms of rejection.

God is trustworthy, and He tells us that He will never leave us or forsake us (see Hebrews 13:5). He also tells us to call him *Abba*, which means *Father*.

"But when the set time had fully come, God sent his Son, born of a woman, born under the law, to redeem those under the law, that we might receive adoption to Sonship. Because you are his sons, God sent the Spirit of his Son into our hearts, the Spirit calls out, "Abba, Father."

(Galatians 4:4-6)

"The Spirit you received does not make you slaves, so that you live in fear again; rather, the Spirit you received brought about your adoption to Sonship. And by him we cry, "Abba, Father."

(Romans 8:15)

Step 11: We must know God's purpose and plan for us.
When we have clear purpose in life, we can navigate through life without being swayed by people or our environment.

"For I know the plans I have for you," declares the LORD, "plans to prosper you and not to harm you, plans to give you hope and a future."

(Jeremiah 29:11)

"For we are God's handiwork, created in Christ Jesus to do good works, which God prepared in advance for us to do."

(Ephesians 2:10)

> *"He has saved us and called us to a holy life—not because of anything we have done but because of his own purpose and grace. This grace was given us in Christ Jesus before the beginning of time."*
>
> (2 Timothy 1:9)

Step 12: Develop a relationship with the Lord by having child-like faith.
Relationship – this is what God wants from us and with us, first and foremost. He wants to develop this relationship on deeper levels throughout our lives.

> *"People were bringing little children to Jesus for him to place his hands on them, but the disciples rebuked them. When Jesus saw this, he was indignant. He said to them, "Let the little children come to me, and do not hinder them, for the kingdom of God belongs to such as these. Truly I tell you, anyone who will not receive the kingdom of God like a little child will never enter it." And he took the children in his arms, placed his hands on them and blessed them."*
>
> (Mark 10:13-16)

* * * * *

The above steps 1-12 can be used as a guideline that you can apply to your unique life. Some wounds will take some time to heal while the other will close up quickly, but remember that God is always at work.

Fasting and prayer helps to deepen our relationship with the Lord as He guides us through the process of transformation to be more like Him, with the help of the Holy Spirit.

> *"And we all, who with unveiled faces contemplate the Lord's glory, are being transformed into his image with ever-increasing joy, which comes from the Lord, who is the Spirit."*
>
> (2 Corinthians 3:18)

CHAPTER 8

FREEDOM FROM AN UNFORGIVING HEART

There is a saying, "Pain is inevitable, but misery is a choice."

An unforgiving heart, bitterness, and resentment go hand in hand. We often witness people's misery because of bitterness in their hearts, and they can look older, unhealthy, and depressed. The problem is that their hearts are full of grudges and bitterness. Their hearts are so unforgiving that they do not experience any changes in their lives, and live without knowing the life and victory and happiness in the Lord.

Many people admit that they find it difficult to forgive others, because their wounds from unfair and unjust treatment are too deep. These people suffer from various emotional issues caused by their wounds and inability to forgive. But God tells us that we must forgive in Matthew 18:21-35.

> *"For if you forgive other people when they sin against you, your heavenly Father will also forgive you. But if you do not forgive others their sins, your Father will not forgive your sins."*
>
> (Matthew 6:14-15)

Meaning of forgiveness

Forgiveness involves an *intentional* decision to let go of resentment and anger. This means that forgiveness is a choice that we make. The best way to understand forgiveness is to look at the cross and realize how much Jesus suffered for our sake, then recall his words, "Father, forgive them, for they do not know what they are doing" (Luke 23:34). Jesus constantly forgives us, and calls us to do the same for others. When we compare the hurts we've received from others to what Jesus experienced, we can forgive even as God forgave us (see Ephesians 4:32).

When we forgive, we:

- Give up our privileges or right to compensation for damages received.
- Decide to understand others.
- Release the debt owed to us.
- Free those who have sinned against us.

God's forgiveness bestowed on sinners is completely different from men forgiving one another. God demands righteousness in exchange for His forgiveness, and this righteousness can only be found through accepting Jesus as our Savior.

- Forgiveness depends on release from debt.
- Forgiveness restores broken relationships between two parties.
- The foundation of God's forgiveness of man's sins is on Christ's death on the cross so that He could redeem all of humanity.
- It is the first step in being restored in the likeness of God.
- It can only be done by the supernatural power of God; God helps us do it.
- When we forgive, God leads us into a deeper level of Christ likeness.

Unforgiving heart originated from the Garden of Eden (see Genesis 3)

In the Garden of Eden, God created mankind, as a man and a woman. Satan approached Eve, the woman, disguised as a snake and deceived Eve to eat the forbidden fruit (disobedience). Eve then convinced Adam to eat the fruit from the tree of knowledge of good and evil, which was forbidden by God, and Adam sinned against God by ignoring God's command. Their eyes were opened from eating the fruit and death entered their lives. From that point on, Adam started blaming Eve ("because of the woman you put here with me … she gave me some fruit from the tree …", vs. 12). This incident changed the relationship between God and man from one of intimacy based on mutual love and understanding, to one based on works, as per a master and servant. Human relationships had also become competitive in nature, caused by jealousy, envy, criticism, resentment, hatred, unforgiving heart, blame, and more.

Forgiveness is God's will

(Matthew 5:23-24; Colossians 3:13-15; Ephesians 4:31-32)

Forgiveness is an essential element that must become a way of life for believers. God calls us to consistently forgive ourselves, forgive others, and forgive Him. God doesn't need our forgiveness but we need to forgive Him in order to release our hearts from blaming him.

> *"For if you forgive other people when they sin against you, your heavenly Father will also forgive you."*
>
> (Matthew 6:14)

In other words, life is about living in harmony with God and our fellow man. We must choose to let go of our bitterness and resentment towards ourselves, others, and God, and unconditionally forgive, regardless of what others have done to us.

> *"And when you stand praying, if you hold anything against anyone, forgive them, so that your Father in heaven may forgive you your sins."*
>
> (Mark 11:25)

> *"Forgive us our sins, for we also forgive everyone who sins against us. And lead us not into temptation."*
>
> (Luke 11:4)

- True freedom and peace come from forgiveness granted to us by the grace of God. Therefore, we also have the duty to forgive those who have hurt us, as God has forgiven us.
- If we refuse to forgive others, we cannot experience and enjoy the grace of God.

> *"See to it that no one falls short of the grace of God and that no bitter root grows up to cause trouble and defile many."*
>
> (Hebrews 12:15)

- Regardless of who has done wrong to us, God wants us to forgive those who have hurt us. When we obey His will, God presents His grace and power to overcome our unforgiving hearts.

Pain and symptoms of not being able to forgive

The pain caused by not being able to forgive is like acid that burns our soul. It destroys the joy and peace of our spirit, and forces us to live under a heavy sense of guilt and judgment. It can make us suffer from physical pain such as headaches, ulcers, indigestion, and insomnia.

Unforgiveness can:

- Weaken our body, physically, emotionally, and spiritually.
- Force us to be critical of others and only to see the negative.
- Make us anxious and oversensitive.
- Have a negative influence in all aspects of life.
- Cause us to repeatedly tell the sob stories of our past.
- Interfere with God's attempt to heal our soul wounds.
- Rob us of our peace with God.
- Blur our judgment and expose us to making foolish decisions.

Reasons why we cannot forgive include:

- We are afraid that we will be ridiculed, if we forgive.
- We are afraid of the other person never knowing the wrong they have done.
- We are afraid of people mistaking who the real sinner is.

As we live out a life based on love, we show that Jesus Christ lives in us, loves us and is loved by us. A person of faith is someone who forgives because Christ forgave them regardless of how the other person may respond.

> *"But God demonstrates his own love for us in this: While we were still sinners, Christ died for us."*
>
> (Romans 5:8)

We are blessed with true peace when we understand God's forgiveness and share it with others.

How to be free from the agony of not being able to forgive

1. We must give up our pride and selfishness.

   > *Then he said to them all: "Whoever wants to be my disciple must deny themselves and take up their cross daily and follow me. For whoever wants to save their life will lose it, but whoever loses their life for me will save it."*
   >
   > (Luke 9:23-24)

   When we humbly pray and fast before God, we crucify our flesh and open our hearts to the Holy Spirit, so that He can work freely in our lives. Instead of arguing about who is at fault, whether it was intentional or unintentional, we need to think of Jesus Christ, who was without sin, but bled on the cross and suffered a tragic death for our sake. Doing so will help us to take full responsibility for our actions.

   Consider the Lord's cross compared to the one you carry. This will help you to obey the will of God to choose to forgive, even if you do not feel like it. When you choose to forgive, God's grace flows in and through us.

   Our forgiveness must be unconditional; conditional forgiveness is only partial.

   Example: *"I do forgive you, but I cannot forget what you have done."*
   "If you apologize first, then I will forgive you."

   However, the Bible tells us:

   > *"This if how we know what love is: Jesus Christ laid down his life for us. And we ought to lay down our lives for our brothers and sisters."*
   >
   > (1 John 3:16)

   After we say we forgive someone, we must not indirectly punish that person by not speaking to them.

   Example: *"You must pay the price first, if you want my forgiveness."*

   We must also stop trying to get even with them, by reminding them of what happened in the past.

> *"Do not take revenge, my dear friends, but leave room for God's wrath, for it is written: "It is mine to avenge; I will repay." says the Lord."*
>
> (Romans 12:19)

2. We must change our focus.
    When our hearts are unforgiving, our thoughts and words can become cynical and critical. The focus we have on those who have hurt us must be shifted to God and His grace.

    > *"Fixing our eyes on Jesus, the pioneer and perfecter of faith. For the joy set before him he endured the cross, scorning its shame, and sat down at the right hand of the throne of God."*
    >
    > (Hebrews 12:2)

    If our forgiveness is real, there really is no need to think about it anymore. If we fast and pray, and seek His guidance humbly and earnestly, God's supernatural power will take us through an amazing transformation and allow us the grace of being able to forgive those who have hurt us. (Fasting helps us maintain our focus.) Forgiveness also releases us from the power of any evil spirit influence in our unforgiving hearts.

3. Recognize that satan wants to keep you in bondage.

    > *"For our struggle is not against flesh and blood, but against the rulers, against the authorities, against the powers of this dark world and against the spiritual forces of evil in the heavenly realms."*
    >
    > (Ephesians 6:12)

    We must understand that satan is our enemy, not our parents, husband, wife, siblings, or anyone else. People remain in the bondage by failing to forgive, and satan uses that bondage to inflict more pain and agony.

    > *"Jesus called his twelve disciples to him and gave them authority to drive out impure spirits and to heal every disease and sickness."*
    >
    > (Matthew 10:1)

Using the authority and power of Jesus Christ that has been given to us, we must put satan and his spiritual forces under our feet. Never forget that he uses people to confront us through their own sense of persecution and prejudice. Unfortunately, even brothers and sisters of faith continue to be abused by satan, often without being aware of it. This is one reason why fasting and prayer must be our weapons of choice in our spiritual warfare. The root of bitterness within us and the yoke of an unforgiving heart must be broken so that we can fully experience the peace and joy of God. Our obedience unleashes the power of God, and gives us the confidence and conviction of who we are and who God is.

4. Follow the ways of Jesus.

> *"But to you who are listening I say: Love your enemies, do good to those who hate you, bless those who curst you, pray for those who mistreat you."*
> (Luke 6:27-28)

Regarding our enemies, Jesus tells us to:

- Love them!
- Bless them!
- Do good to them!
- Pray for them!

This is not possible without the grace of God; it is in our nature to strike back when injustice is done against us. For example, hatred, which brings an intense desire for revenge, ends up hurting US instead of those we have targeted. In other words, we will be the biggest victim of our own hatred, when all is said and done.

Breaking the curse of revenge is the only way to be free from the agony of not being able to forgive. We must choose to forgive for OUR benefit. Not being able to forgive is like a shadow of death following us around.

How do we start forgiving?

First, start by praying for those who have hurt you. It will be difficult at first, but you must keep trying. Remember, forgiveness is a choice, not an emotion. Consider that

Jesus forgave all who came against Him, while in excruciating pain and hanging on the cross (see Luke 23:34).

Second, confess to God your hurt-filled thoughts and words of condemnation targeted toward those who have hurt you, and ask for, and receive, His forgiveness.

Third, forgive by speaking out individual names.

Fourth, Ask God to heal your wounds and help you to love those who have hurt you. Whenever painful memories make their way into your heart, a key is to say out loud, "I do not condemn them; I bless them." Then ask God to bless them as He sees fit.

When you continue to pray this way, the power and grace of God will work within you and your wounded heart will gradually be healed. As time passes, you will be able to forgive naturally, rather than having to work hard at it. When you truly forgive those who have caused you pain, you can bless them, instead of cursing them with harm.

CHAPTER 9

BREAKING SOUL TIES

A soul tie is an emotional and spiritual connection between two people. It can be formed through relationships and interactions with individuals, such as family members, friends, co-workers, romantic partners, and even pets.

Good soul tie

The relationship between parents and their children, husband and wife, and among disciples of Christ are examples of good soul ties. The Law of Christ is to "love your neighbor as yourself." This commandment is based on agape (unconditional) love and is a relationship that God approves of.

> *"Carry each other's burdens, and in this way, you will fulfill the law of Christ."*
>
> (Galatians 6:2)

> *If you really keep the royal law found in Scripture, "Love you neighbor as yourself, you are doing right."*
>
> (James 2:8)

1. Union of marriage

    > *In this same way, husbands ought to love their wives as their own bodies. He who loves his wife loves himself. After all, no one ever hated their own body, but they feed and care for their body, just as Christ does the church—for we are members of his body. "For this reason a man will leave*

his father and mother and be united to his wife, and the two will become one flesh."

(Ephesians 5:28-31)

God's intention for marriage is for a man and a woman to be united as one. Sex within a marriage is an expression of their love, uniting them as one.

"So they are no longer two, but on flesh. Therefore what God has joined together, let no one separate."

(Matthew 19:6)

2. Soul tie through friendship

   "After David had finished talking with Saul, Jonathan became one in spirit with David, and he loved him as himself."

   (1 Samuel 18:1)

Jonathan honored David so much that he gave up his right to the throne of the kingdom of Israel.

3. Soul tie between parents and their children
   Read Genesis 44: 20-30.

   Jacob mourned for his son, Joseph, when he thought Joseph had been killed. Every parent knows that they are instantly tied to their newborn, and the newborn becomes instantly tied to their parents.

4. Soul tie among believers

   "From him the whole body, joined and held together by every supporting ligament, grows and builds itself up in love, as each part does its work."

   (Ephesians 4:16)

Godly soul ties among believers help the Body of Christ to grow in healthy ways.

Ungodly soul ties

Ungodly soul ties corrupt the hearts of individuals. They are formed based on selfish desires. Satan can only work within the opportunities and boundaries we allow him, and ungodly soul times are an open door for him to walk through.

1. Formation of an ungodly soul tie through adultery

   Do you not know that he who unites himself with a prostitute is one with her in body? For it is said, "The two will become one flesh."
   (1 Corinthians 6:16)

   - Extramarital sex forms an evil soul tie. Sex in marriage is a God-given blessing, a good soul tie, that unites husband and wife as one. However, extramarital affairs and the sexual immorality forms an ungodly soul tie.
   - Extramarital sex opens the door for seducing and seductive spirits to enter into our souls. Today's society publicly tolerates extramarital sex, but the law of God allows sex only between spouses.
   - Sexual relationships before marriage or outside of marriage are adultery in God's eyes.

   An evil soul tie that is sexual in nature does not only happen between man and woman, but also between people of the same sex.

   "Because of this, God gave them over to shameful lusts. Even their women exchanged natural sexual relations for unnatural ones. In the same way the men also abandoned natural relations with women and were inflamed with lust for one another. Men committed shameful acts with other men and received in themselves the due penalty for their error."
   (Romans 1:26-27)

   Sadly, mankind has become so corrupt, that bestiality—sex between a human and an animal—has become common in some circles. A corrupted soul tie is formed in an immoral relationship between man and beast.

2. Soul ties with evil associations

   "Do not be misled: "Bad company corrupts good character."
   (1 Corinthians 15:33)

   Friendships have a great influence over us. Therefore, who we choose to become friends with is a very important issue. Soul ties with a wrong person is a shortcut for us to fall into satan's traps.

   "In the paths of the wicked are snares and pitfalls, but those who would preserve their life stay far from them."
   (Proverbs 22:5)

   "Do not make friends with a hot-tempered person, do not associate with one easily angered, or you may learn their ways and get yourself ensnared."
   (Proverbs 22:24-25)

3. Unhealthy soul ties with family
   Satan employs various tactics to corrupt good soul ties between family members. Parents who control their adult children's lives and adult children who rely on mom and dad to solve their problems may deal with co-dependency issues which can be a sign of an unhealthy soul tie.

   "For this reason, a man will leave his father and mother and be united to his wife, and the two will become one flesh."
   (Ephesians 5:31)

   When a man leaves his parents, he does not sever all ties with them. Instead, he is now independent enough to take responsibility for his life and his spouse. His relationship with his parents has changed to a different role on a more mature level.

4. Soul tie with the dead
   When a close friend or family member dies, there is a normal grieving process, part of which is breaking the soul tie with that person. Mourning for a certain period

of time is necessary, for example, Moses was mourned for a month; Jacob was mourned for a week.

> *"The Israelites grieved for Moses in the plains of Moab thirty days, until the time of weeping and mourning was over."*
> (Deuteronomy 34:8)

> *"When they reached the threshing floor of Atad, near the Jordan, they lamented loudly and bitterly; and there Joseph observed a seven-day period of mourning for his father."*
> (Genesis 50:10)

However, mourning that continues for months and even years show that the soul tie with the dead person remains intact. This can be an open door for a spirit of heaviness, depression, or anxiety to harm our soul.

5. Evil soul tie within a church
   When the spirit of criticism comes against the leaders of a church and causes a division within the local body, an ungodly soul tie is formed between those who come against leadership and is demonstrated through gossip, slander, and discord.

   > *"While our presentable parts need no special treatment. But God has put the body together, giving greater honor to the parts that lacked it, so that there should be no division in the body, but that its parts should have equal concern for each other."*
   > (1 Corinthians 12:24-25)

   When the leaders of the church put themselves ahead of Jesus Christ, who is the head of the church, an ungodly soul tie is formed with themselves. They become prideful, and think they are the answer to everything, and the only ones capable of making decisions or giving guidance. They have lost track of "Not I that lives but Christ that lives in me" (see Galatians 2:20). Therefore, spiritual leaders must look to Christ, who is the head of His church, and obey Him. This allows spiritual leaders to maintain a good relationship with their flocks.

   As church members, we put Christ first by not exalting ourselves over the church leaders, but being willing to humbly follow and obey our leaders.

For when one says, "I follow Paul," and another, "I follow Apollos," are you not mere human beings? What after all, is Apollos? And what is Paul? Only servants, through whom you came to believe—as the Lord has assigned to each his task.

(1 Corinthians 3:4-5)

Cause of an ungodly soul tie

God has set boundaries in human relationships that apply to marital relationships, business relationships, friendships, and among many others. When these boundaries are respected and protected, good relationships are maintained. However, when these boundaries are crossed, satan puts his strategies to work so that an ungodly soul tie is formed in these relationships.

Power of soul ties

The power of soul ties can be gauged by two words: unity and fellowship.

1. Unity
    a. Marriage

    "For this reason, a man will leave his father and mother and be united to his wife, and the two will become one flesh."

    (Ephesians 5:31)

    "So, they are no longer two, but one flesh. Therefore, what God has joined together, let no one separate."

    (Matthew 19:6)

    God intended marriage to be pure and healthy. Unfortunately, sexual immorality, co-dependency, and domination will corrupt this relationship and create an ungodly soul tie.

b. Church

   "From him the whole body, joined and held together by every supporting ligament, grows and builds itself up in love, as each part does its work."
   (Ephesians 4:16)

   The fact that the church is one body means that every part has a great influence on each other.

   "Your boasting is not good. Don't you know that a little yeast leavens the whole batch of dough get rid of the old yeast, so that you may be a new unleavened bath – as you really are. For Christ, our Passover lamb has been sacrificed."
   (1 Corinthians 5:6-7)

c. The Lord

   "But whoever is united with the Lord is one with him in Spirit."
   (1 Corinthians 6:17)

   As adultery is having sex outside of marriage, we can also commit "spiritual" adultery against the Lord. Idolatry and all other worship rituals are considered spiritual adultery. When we seek spiritual abilities, knowledge, and wisdom from any other source—i.e., a fortune teller, a psychic, false cults, or occult experiences—other than God and His Word, we are committing spiritual adultery.

   "So Israel yoked themselves to the Baal of Peor. And the Lord's anger burned against them."
   (Numbers 25:3)

   Just like physical adultery, spiritual adultery forms an evil soul tie.

2. Fellowship
    a. Fellowship with Christ through His Sacrifice
       Fellowship in Greek means communion. Our fellowship as believers is in Christ.

       "Is not the cup of thanksgiving for which we give thanks a participation in the body of Christ? And is not the bread that we break a participation in the body of Christ? Because there is one loaf, we, who are many, are one body, for we all share the one loaf."
       (1 Corinthians 10:16-17)

    b. Fellowship with satan through occult worshipping
       To participate in activities related to idol worship such as hypnosis, astrology, or following horoscopes is to follow other gods, and such action will bring the Lord's judgment.

       "Therefore, my dear friends flee from idolatry."
       (1 Corinthians 10:14)

       "You cannot drink the cup of the Lord and the cup of the demons too; you cannot have a part in both the Lord's table and the table of demons. Are we trying to arouse the Lord's jealousy? Are we stronger than he?"
       (1 Corinthians 10:21-22)

       "But their idols are silver and gold, made by human hands. They have mouths, but cannot speak, eyes, but cannot see. They have ears but cannot hear, noses, but cannot smell. They have hands, but cannot feel, feet, but cannot walk, nor can they utter a sound with their throats. Those who make them will be like them, and so will all who trust in them."
       (Psalms 115:4-8)

How to break an evil soul tie

An evil soul tie can be broken when we repent of our actions and turn back to God. To disobey God's Word is to sin against Him. Even if it was done out of ignorance, the process of repentance and forgiveness is necessary.

We must get rid of all evil roots that have brought about these evil soul ties (see Hebrews 12:15 as an example). We must renounce satan's influence over our lives, and break his power by the name and blood of Jesus.

In the name of the Lord Jesus Christ, order all evil spirits that have been working through these evil soul ties to leave you. Call out each one until all are broken. Call out the names of all sexual partners and break the ungodly ties formed from these inappropriate relationships. Bestiality, incest, unethical relationship among members of the church, participation in idolatry, fortune tellers, hypnosis, contract of blood, any impure oaths, all involvement in false cults or the occult, and more must be rooted out.

Always remember to forgive all who have hurt you, as part of breaking the ungodly soul tie. Forgiveness is necessary, if you are to break all ungodly soul ties and deny satan's access into your life. Rebuke all evil spirits in the name of Jesus Christ!

CHAPTER 10

THE POWER OF THE LIE

by Pastor Larry Fannin

Isaiah 58:8[3]

> *"Then your light shall break forth like the morning, Your healing shall spring forth speedily, And your righteousness shall go before you; The glory of the L*ORD *shall be your rear guard."*

- **What the Holy Spirit does**
  The Holy Spirit, the Spirit of Truth, shines the light of Truth upon our lives, when the ruler of sins and darkness has darkened our hearts and minds.

Colossians 1:13-14

> *"He has delivered us from the power of darkness and conveyed us into the kingdom of the Son of His love, in whom we have redemption through His blood, the forgiveness of sins."*
>
> (emphasis, mine)

- **Purpose**
  Satan's purpose is to blind our minds through the power of the lie so we will not be able to seek or serve the Lord.

---

[3] All scriptures in this chapter are NKJV.

2 Corinthians 4:4

"whose minds the god of this age has blinded, who do not believe, lest the light of the gospel of the glory of Christ, who is the image of God, should shine on them."

Why we continue to fail in life

Despite having entered into the Kingdom of Light after being born again, there are areas within our soul and spirit that are in bondage to, controlled by, or under the influence of evil spirits.

If we are continually swayed by doubt, unbelief, fear, anxiety, or other sins, then we cannot help but continue to struggle and fail in particular areas of life. Therefore, we must first understand what the lie is and how it has "blinded our minds" (see 2 Corinthians 4:4), so that we can believe the truth of God's Word to reveal our darkness and bring us into the light of God's love and acceptance.

As a little match lights up an entire room so we can move around, we can only triumph when our inner being is filled with the light of truth as the Holy Spirit reveals blind spots in our life.

1. **Power of Lies**

    When you are bound by the power of a lie, the truth looks like the lie and the lie becomes the truth. We exchange the truth for the lie. This is because the father of lies has covered our eyes so that we become blind to the Truth.

    John 8:44

    "You are of your father the devil, and the desires of your father you want to do. He was a murderer from the beginning, and does not stand in the truth, because there is no truth in him. When he speaks a lie, he speaks from his own resources, for he is a liar and the father of it."

    Proverbs 23:7

    "For as he thinks in his heart, so is he. "Eat and drink!" he says to you, But his heart is not with you."

We have come to believe his lies as the truth through his deception. We have planted his seed of lies in our hearts as if they are the truth, which has caused blind spots.

With the help of the Holy Spirit, we must put the truth and the lie in their right places through the Word of God.

Romans 1:25

"who exchanged the truth of God for the lie and worshiped and served the creature rather than the Creator, who is blessed forever. Amen."

2. **Why we are unable to put the truth and the lie in the right places**
   Our sins and our darkest secrets have been hidden so well that they are difficult to bring to the light. We can be free when we admit to our hidden sins and confess them to God.

Psalm 139:23-24

"Search me, O God, and know my heart; Try me, and know my anxieties; And see if there is any wicked way in me, And lead me in the way everlasting."

The Lord reveals our sins to heal us

When we give ourselves to the Lord to examine us, He shows us places that we have not seen before. This can be an extremely painful experience as it requires a vulnerable process of having to remember things we buried deep in our subconscious and never wanted to think about again.

1. **David's secret sin**
   David's heart was before God until he became careless and committed the sin of adultery with Bathsheba. However, David's sin was not a result of one mistake for one night. When his inner darkness hidden inside was given a right set of circumstances, it seized the opportunity and revealed itself. God revealed David's sin in order to heal him.

James 1:14-15

> *"But each one is tempted when he is drawn away by his own desires and enticed. Then, when desire has conceived, it gives birth to sin; and sin, when it is full-grown, brings forth death."*

It is the "seed of lies" within us that makes us stumble. Therefore, we need to understand how satan deceives us, how he plants these seeds in us, and how he darkens our hearts.

2. **Places where the seed of lies goes to work**
   - Inside our minds (using the wounds and pains caused by trauma experienced in our childhood and evil thoughts)
   - Through past experiences (abuse, physical and sexual abuse, neglected by parents, severe child abuse, verbal abuse, etc.)

The seed grows

- It has a tremendous impact on the formation of our character and emotional health and goes on to destroy our self-image and belief system. As a result, we do not become transformed into the likeness of Christ; instead, we have formed a false self-image and are unable to see who we truly are as God creation.

Loving God Under Trials

James 1:12

> *"Blessed is the man who endures temptation; for when he has been approved, he will receive the crown of life which the Lord has promised to those who love Him."*

The lie is exposed through a period of testing. Iron can only become steel after spending a long time in the fire. If we depend on the Lord and persevere in times of trials where our weaknesses are exposed, God will turn our weaknesses into our strengths. God's will is to heal us and make us whole again.

James 1:13

> *Let no one say when he is tempted, "I am tempted by God"; for God cannot be tempted by evil, nor does He Himself tempt anyone.*

- God allows our faith to be tested, but He does not tempt us to do evil or any sin.
- Satan tempts us to make us stumble to lead us into sin.

James 1:14-15

> *"But each one is tempted when he is drawn away by his own desires and enticed. Then, when desire has conceived, it gives birth to sin; and sin, when it is full-grown, brings forth death."*

Satan stimulates our inner desire with his enticements. What causes us to embrace his enticements is always within us (greed, sexual temptation, pride, satisfaction of our desires, envy, etc.). When Jesus was tempted by satan, there was nothing satan could grab onto. Why? Because there was nothing in Jesus that could have caused Him to sin. He was tempted but was without sin (see Hebrews 4:15).

Even if we are born again and become a new creation through the grace of Jesus Christ, we will continue to be a slave to our sinful nature if we do not believe the Truth and receive forgiveness and healing from the Lord.

Seed of satan's ideas

The moment we bite satan's bait, it becomes sin and will put its root down and give birth to acts of sin. Until we resist their temptations and rebuke their hold on our lives, evil spirits will continue to tempt us and deceive us, disguising their actions, so we become hardened to sin. We end up blinded to "the wiles of the devil" (see Ephesians 6:11) because we have fallen into his trap of temptation.

Matthew 5:28

> *"But I say to you that whoever looks at a woman to lust for her has already committed adultery with her in his heart."*

When satan reels us in, our minds have already been blinded, our hearts have already been captured, we have already started down a path of destruction. When we bite the bait, satan gains greater control over our lives. In our struggle against evil spiritual forces, we will be worn down, and our body and spirit become weary. Only the conviction of the Holy Spirit can help us recognize our sins, and only the forgiveness of Jesus can cleanse us from all impurity.

Sin begins in our hearts before any action is taken

This is because there is hidden, wounded spots within us, and we are weak and bound by our fleshly desires. These things will come together to create a fertile soil for the seed of temptation to grow. Therefore, we must pull any and all spiritual weeds growing in the garden of our minds.

3. **Satan's tactic is to deceive**
   Satan's tactics have never changed from the Creation, as we read in Genesis 2 and 3.

   2 Corinthians 11:3

   > *"But I fear, lest somehow, as the serpent deceived Eve by his craftiness, so your minds may be corrupted from the simplicity that is in Christ."*

How does satan deceive?

- He draws our attention to control us.
- He asks questions to encourage us to act.
- He considers it a success when we answer his questions as he had gotten our attention.

We also deceive ourselves

James 1:22

> *"But be doers of the word, and not hearers only, deceiving yourselves."*

Galatians 6:3

> *"For if anyone thinks himself to be something, when he is nothing, he deceives himself."*

Deception is thinking we know more than God. God is always right and always has our best interests in mind. Only through obeying the Word of God and acting on it can we discern between the truth and the lie.

King Saul lost his blessings and authority because he did not obey. When the Prophet Samuel stood before him, Saul blamed others instead of admitting to his sins and taking responsibility for his actions. When the Holy Spirit rebukes us, we must first be willing to admit to our responsibility, instead of hiding our sins from God. Only then will He take us on a path of restoration.

God will rebuke you when you intentionally disobey Him

Galatians 6:7-8

> *"Do not be deceived, God is not mocked; for whatever a man sows, that he will also reap. For he who sows to his flesh will of the flesh reap corruption, but he who sows to the Spirit will of the Spirit reap everlasting life."*

Romans 8:5

> *"For those who live according to the flesh set their minds on the things of the flesh, but those who live according to the Spirit, the things of the Spirit."*

We reap what we sow. When we sow to the desires of the flesh, we will reap consequences of the flesh; when we sow to the desires of the Spirit, we will reap the rewards of the Spirit. We must be able to sow God's good seeds in the fertile soil of our heart, so they can produce good fruits of life dedicated to God.

The ways of Jesus

We must utilize the ways of Jesus, if we are not to be deceived by satan.

- Jesus overcame temptation with the Word of God. (see Matthew 4)
- Jesus never got into a discussion with satan.

How do we avoid satan's deception?

1. Become doers of the Word of God, instead of merely listening to the Word.
2. Admit to your sins, take full responsibility for them, and confess to the Lord immediately.
3. Do not blame others; forgive and bless them.
4. Continue to plant the seed of the Word of God in our hearts and minds.
5. Obey God unconditionally.
6. Aim to please God in all you do.

CHAPTER 11

UNBELIEF AND FAITH

by Pastor Larry Fannin

What is unbelief?

Unbelief refers to being deceived by the lies of satan and evil spirits. When we are deceived, we are believing the voices of satan as more trustworthy than the Word of God or the leading of the Holy Spirit.

Definition of unbelief

Unbelief can be defined as acting on man's own reasons and intentions, instead of believing in and obeying the Word of God.

Origins of unbelief

It started with Adam and Eve; they trusted satan words over God's commands.

Genesis 3:4-6[4]

> *"You will not certainly die," the serpent said to the woman. "For God knows that when you eat from it your eyes will be opened, and you will be like God, knowing good and evil." When the woman saw that the fruit of the tree was good for food and pleasing to the eye, and also desirable*

---

[4] All Scriptures in this chapter are NIV.

for gaining wisdom, she took some and ate it. She also gave some to her husband, who was with her, and he ate it."

- False teachings and traditions of men.

Matthew 15:3

Jesus replied, "And why do you break the command of God for the sake of your tradition?"

- When our prayer is not answered.

Habakkuk 1:2-4

Habakkuk's Complaint
"How long, Lord, must I call for help, but you do not listen? Or cry out to you, "Violence!" but you do not save? Why do you make me look at injustice? Why do you tolerate wrongdoing? Destruction and violence are before me; there is strife, and conflict abounds. Therefore the law is paralyzed, and justice never prevails. The wicked hem in the righteous, so that justice is perverted."

- We hold ourselves hostage by limiting God.

Luke 1:18-2

Zechariah asked the angel, "How can I be sure of this? I am an old man and my wife is well along in years." The angel said to him, "I am Gabriel. I stand in the presence of God, and I have been sent to speak to you and to tell you this good news. And now you will be silent and not able to speak until the day this happens, because you did not believe my words, which will come true at their appointed time." Meanwhile, the people were waiting for Zechariah and wondering why he stayed so long in the temple. When he came out, he could not speak to them. They realized he had seen a vision in the temple, for he kept making signs to them but remained unable to speak. When his time of service was completed, he returned home.

Genesis 18:12

> *So Sarah laughed to herself as she thought, "After I am worn out and my lord is old, will I now have this pleasure?"*

- When we close our hearts to God and resent Him because of our spiritual wounds.

Damages caused by unbelief

- Your prayer will go unanswered.

James 1:6-8

> *"But when you ask, you must believe and not doubt, because the one who doubts is like a wave of the sea, blown and tossed by the wind. That person should not expect to receive anything from the Lord. Such a person is double-minded and unstable in all they do."*

- You will not be blessed and will not be able to fulfill your vision.

1 Samuel 13:13-14

> *"You have done a foolish thing," Samuel said. "You have not kept the command the Lord your God gave you; if you had, he would have established your kingdom over Israel for all time. But now your kingdom will not endure; the Lord has sought out a man after his own heart and appointed him ruler of his people, because you have not kept the Lord's command."*

- You will not have joy and peace. You may become depressed and insecure, or anxious and impatient, so you act before consulting God and waiting for His response. (1 Samuel 13:8-14; 16:14)
- You will not trust in the Word of God. (John 6:40-58; 64-65)
- Your relationship with God is severed and you lose your authority as a child of God. (Genesis 3:1-24)
- You will be filled with doubt and fear, and suffer through illnesses and insomnia.

- You will become indecisive.
- You will be cold, loveless and lack passion.
- You will fear death and will be unsure of your salvation.
- You will not know the real Gospel, but become legalistic. (Luke 6:6-11)

What does God say about unbelief?

- He finds it incredulous.

    Mark 6:6

    "He was amazed at their lack of faith."

- He says we are double minded and unstable in all we do.

    James 1:8

    "Such a person is double-minded and unstable in all they do."

- He tells us not to become a person who merely listens to the Word and deceives himself; instead become a person who does what it says.

    James 1:22

    "Do not merely listen to the word, and so deceive yourselves. Do what it says."

- He says not doing what the Word says even after listening to it would be like looking at his face in a mirror but immediately forgets what he looks like.

    James 1:23-24

    "Anyone who listens to the word but does not do what it says is like someone who looks at his face in a mirror and, after looking at himself, goes away and immediately forgets what he looks like."

- He says faith without action is dead.

    James 2:26

    "As the body without the spirit is dead, so faith without deeds is dead."

- He warns us not to have a sinful unbelieving heart.

    Hebrews 3:12

    "See to it, brothers and sisters, that none of you has a sinful, unbelieving heart that turns away from the living God."

- He called the ten spies evil, but not Joshua and Caleb.

    Numbers 13:26-14:5

    Report on the Exploration
    They came back to Moses and Aaron and the whole Israelite community at Kadesh in the Desert of Paran. There they reported to them and to the whole assembly and showed them the fruit of the land. They gave Moses this account: "We went into the land to which you sent us, and it does flow with milk and honey! Here is its fruit. But the people who live there are powerful, and the cities are fortified and very large. We even saw descendants of Anak there. The Amalekites live in the Negev; the Hittites, Jebusites and Amorites live in the hill country; and the Canaanites live near the sea and along the Jordan." Then Caleb silenced the people before Moses and said, "We should go up and take possession of the land, for we can certainly do it." But the men who had gone up with him said, "We can't attack those people; they are stronger than we are." And they spread among the Israelites a bad report about the land they had explored. They said, "The land we explored devours those living in it. All the people we saw there are of great size. We saw the Nephilim there (the descendants of Anak come from the Nephilim). We seemed like grasshoppers in our own eyes, and we looked the same to them."

> *The People Rebel*
> *That night all the members of the community raised their voices and wept aloud. All the Israelites grumbled against Moses and Aaron, and the whole assembly said to them, "If only we had died in Egypt! Or in this wilderness! Why is the Lord bringing us to this land only to let us fall by the sword? Our wives and children will be taken as plunder. Wouldn't it be better for us to go back to Egypt?" And they said to each other, "We should choose a leader and go back to Egypt." Then Moses and Aaron fell face down in front of the whole Israelite assembly gathered there.*

- He says the mouth speaks what the heart is full of.

Matthew 12:34

> *"You brood of vipers, how can you who are evil say anything good? For the mouth speaks what the heart is full of."*

What is Faith?

Faith believes that God always does what He promises.

Hebrews 11:1

> *"Now faith is confidence in what we hope for and assurance about what we do not see."*

Results of acting on our faith

- We receive the result of our faith, in other words, salvation of our soul.
- We receive the earth as inheritance like Joshua and Caleb did. (Joshua 14:12-14)
- Our children and I will be blessed. (Deuteronomy 30:1-6)
- We give glory to God as we will bear an abundance of fruit in our life that has been enriched and share it with our neighbors.
- We become friends with the Lord. (John 15:14)
- We become courageous and effectively use the authority Jesus has given us. (Matthew 28:18-20)

- We will work passionately, filled with joy and the Holy Spirit. (i.e., the disciples in the book of Acts)
- We will fulfill God's vision. (Samuel, Daniel, Paul, etc.)
- We will be rewarded in the Kingdom of Heaven. (2 Timothy 4:7-8)

Why we need faith

We cannot please God without faith.

Hebrews 11:6

> *"And without faith it is impossible to please God, because anyone who comes to him must believe that he exists and that he rewards those who earnestly seek him."*

What it means to have faith towards God

Our faith towards God reveals our attitude toward Him. Some may hate Him, some may refuse Him, some may fear Him. The right attitude towards God is to believe that He is our protector and defender, and He will fulfill his promises to us, regardless of our circumstances, regardless of what our thoughts and emotions may be, regardless of whether we are able to see Him, hear Him, or touch Him.

Biblical Example

- Abraham had faith towards God. (Genesis 15:1-6)
- Paul had faith towards God. (Acts 27:21-44)

How can we have faith?

Faith is a gift of God.

Romans 12:3

> *"For by the grace given me I say to every one of you: Do not think of yourself more highly than you ought, but rather think of yourself with sober judgment, in accordance with the faith God has distributed to each of you."*

Every born-again person has a foundation of faith. The more you listen to the Word of God, the stronger faith you will receive.

Romans 10:17

> *"Consequently, faith comes from hearing the message, and the message is heard through the word about Christ."*

What kind of faith does God demand of us?

The Bible shows us that even faith as small as a mustard seed will make anything possible.

Matthew 17:20

> *He replied, "Because you have so little faith. Truly I tell you, if you have faith as small as a mustard seed, you can say to this mountain, 'Move from here to there,' and it will move. Nothing will be impossible for you."*

Is faith part of Christ's teaching?

Yes. Faith towards God is the second part of Christ's teaching in the book of Hebrews. Faith, like repentance, is necessary in all areas of life when we walk with God.

Hebrews 6:1

> *"Therefore let us move beyond the elementary teachings about Christ and be taken forward to maturity, not laying again the foundation of repentance from acts that lead to death, and of faith in God."*

Can faith be our weapon?

Yes. When the power of evil rises against us in our heart, we can destroy it by using our faith.

Ephesians 6:16

> *"In addition to all this, take up the shield of faith, with which you can extinguish all the flaming arrows of the evil one."*

Resolution to unbelief

1. Honestly admit to your unbelief and confess to the Lord.
   - To be ashamed of unbelief and hide it is to protect the evil spirit, which will keep us in the midst of unbelief and curse.
   - You must completely repent all things done in unbelief, deceived by the lies of satan and evil spirits.
   - You must drive out all evil spirits hiding in our unbelief.
   - You must continue searching for the Word of God and proclaim it until your unbelief is renewed as a complete faith.
2. Proclaim the Word of God.
   - I have been chosen by Him according to His plan. (Ephesians 1:11)
   - I have the authority of Jesus Christ. (Luke 10:19)
   - Jesus redeemed us from the curse of the Law through His cross and allowed me to receive Abraham's blessings. (Galatians 3:13-14)
   - I am an heir of God and will share in Christ's glory. (Romans 8:17)
   - I am the caretaker of all creatures on the earth. (Genesis 2:15)
   - Jesus is always with me and protects me. (Isaiah 41:10; 43:1-2)
   - Jesus always intercedes for me and guides me. (Romans 8:34 Psalms 23:1-6)
   - My body is the temple in which the Holy Spirit dwells. (1 Corinthians 3:16)
   - He tells the weak to say I am strong by the grace of God. (2 Corinthians 12:9-10)
3. Act on the Word of God with faith and make His promises yours.
   - Fight the good fight of faith. (1 Timothy 6:12)
   - Joshua and Caleb went into the land of Canaan by perfectly trusting God. (Numbers 14:24)
   - God will protect those whose minds are steadfast. (Isaiah 26:3)
   - It is with your heart that you believe and are justified, and it is with your mouth that you confess your faith and are saved. (Romans 10:10)
   - Faith is assurance about what we do not see. (Hebrews 11:1)

- Whatever you ask for in prayer, believe that you have received it and it will be yours. (Mark 11:23-24)
- Do not lean on your own understanding, but trust in the Lord with all your heart. (Psalms 44:6, Proverbs 3:5-6)
- The righteous will live by faith. (Romans 1:17, Habakkuk 2:4)
- Everything is possible for the one who believes. (Mark 9:23)
- If you believe, you will see the glory of God. (John 11:40)
- Do not put your trust in princes, in human beings, who cannot save. (Psalms 146:3-5)

Unbelief has its foundation in our emotions and changes our direction of life. But if you hold firm to your confession of faith that Jesus is the Lord, Jesus will lift your life to that of success.

Do not attempt to resolve all of your problems at once; be patient and rejoice in your progress as your faith grows. If you make a mistake, you can start over. Do start over. Get up again and again. Only then will you be successful.

For though the righteous fall seven times, they rise again, but the wicked stumble when calamity strikes. (Proverbs 24:16)

- Build a strong wall of faith so a thief called unbelief will not enter.
- Always be filled with the Holy Spirit. (Ephesians 5:18)

CHAPTER 12

DISCOVERING YOUR SELF-WORTH IN CHRIST

There are countless people who do not like themselves because of their feelings of self-rejection. Many types of psychological issues have their roots in their childhood experiences. We must understand why so many young people are lost in their pain. They want to be loved and recognized. They want to be accepted for they are; however, current social conditions and pressures makes it impossible for them to grow up and become who they are meant to be, according to God's plan and purpose.

> *"Before I formed you in the womb I knew[a] you, before you were born I set you apart; I appointed you as a prophet to the nations."*
>
> (Jeremiah 1:5)

> 13 *For you created my inmost being;*
> *you knit me together in my mother's womb.*
> 14 *I praise you because I am fearfully and wonderfully made;*
> *your works are wonderful,*
> *I know that full well.*
> 15 *My frame was not hidden from you*
> *when I was made in the secret place,*
> *when I was woven together in the depths of the earth.*
> 16 *Your eyes saw my unformed body;*
> *all the days ordained for me were written in your book*
> *before one of them came to be.*
> 17 *How precious to me are your thoughts, God!*
> *How vast is the sum of them!*

> *18 Were I to count them,*
> *they would outnumber the grains of sand—*
> *when I awake, I am still with you.*
>
> (Psalm 139:13-18)

To live a happy, rewarding, and worthwhile life on this earth, we must first establish a Godly self-image based on the Word of God, and know our value in Christ, by understanding our Creator is the all-powerful God. When we fully accept that we are loved by Him and recognized as His children, we will be able to accept ourselves as forgiven children of God.

> *"For I am the least of the apostles and do not even deserve to be called an apostle, because I persecuted the church of God. But by the grace of God, I am what I am, and his grace to me was not without effect. No, I worked harder than all of them – yet no I, but the grace of God that was with me."*
>
> (1 Corinthians 15:9-10)

We may be overweight or we may be skinny. But we would be wrong to think that God would love us any less because of our appearance. God does not judge based on appearances; rather He looks at our heart.

> *"But the Lord said to Samuel, "Do not consider his appearance or his height for I have rejected him. The Lord does not look at the things people look at. People look at the outward appearance, but the Lord looks at the heart."*
>
> (1 Samuel 16:7)

Sometimes we ask ourselves questions such as, "Why is my nose so small? Why am I so tall or so short? Why is my face so long or so round? Why did I have to be born like this?"

> *"But who are you, a human being, to talk back to God? "Shall what is formed say to the one who formed it, 'Why did you make me like this?" Does not the potter have the right to make out of the same lump of clay some pottery for special purposes and some for common use?"*
>
> (Romans 9:20-21)

"For you created my inmost being you knit me together in my mother's womb. I praise you because I am fearfully and wonderfully made; your works are wonderful. I know that full well. My frame was not hidden from you when I was made in the secret place, when I was woven together in the depths of the earth. Your eyes saw my unformed body; all the days ordained for me were written in your book before one of them came to be."
(Psalms 139:13-16)

"Jesus replied: love the lord your God with all your heart and with all your soul and with all your mind. This is the first and greatest commandment. And the second is like it: love your neighbor as yourself."
(Matthew 22:37-39)

To discover your true value, you must first be convinced of God's forgiveness and forgive yourself, regardless of what mistakes you have made or sins you have committed.

"If we confess our sins, he is faithful and just and will forgive us our sins and purify us from all unrighteousness."
(1 John 1:9)

"Therefore, there is now no condemnation for those who are in Christ Jesus."
(Romans 8:1)

We commit sin because of our sinful nature. There are many instances in our lives that are regretful, and when we come to this realization, we also realize that our flesh is weak. We sin because we cannot control our carnal nature, and we need the power of the Holy Spirit to help us not to sin.

"Brothers and sisters, I do not consider myself yet to have taken hold of it. But one thing I do: Forgetting what is behind and straining toward what is ahead."
(Philippians 3:13)

The Apostle Paul had a past like no other. He persecuted Christians and considered the stoning death of Stephen justified. He was on his way to Damascus to kill all

Christians he could find. But after he was transformed, Paul did not keep himself trapped in a guilty conscience that was shackled to his past sins. Like Paul, we must also focus on our future with God's purpose in mind we must never look back.

> *"Their sins and lawless acts I will remember no more."*
> (Hebrews 10:17)

To live in pain because we cannot forgive what God has already forgiven is no different from trying to become God to ourselves.

God loves us so much that He sent His only son, Jesus, to die on the cross so that He could redeem us from all sins and move us from the kingdom of darkness to the kingdom of light. Therefore, we must receive God's forgiveness if we are to move forward in Kingdom living—living according to God's Word and His principles, and receiving all of His benefits—instead of simply going through the motions.

Don't compare yourself to others.

> *"We do not dare to classify or compare ourselves with some who commend themselves. When they measure themselves by themselves and compare themselves with themselves, they are not wise. We, however, will not boast beyond proper limits, but will confine our boasting to the sphere of service God himself has assigned to us, a sphere that also includes you."*
> (2 Corinthians 10:12-13)

God has created each one of us unique; there is no one exactly like you. There has never been anyone like you, nor will there be another you again. In the family of God, there is no one who is better or worse; we are all equal in His sight. If we are to judge our value based on the standards of this world, we will never live a happy and fulfilling life; we will continue to be disappointed and live in despair and fear.

What is success? Money, a beautiful house, or a nice car? Even if you have everything this world can possibly offer, it is worthless if you do not have the joy and peace in your heart that knowing Jesus Christ brings. True success is to be faithful to the work you have been entrusted with, and using your God-given talent and abilities for His glory. When we do not compare ourselves to others and instead use our talent and abilities for God and His purposes, we can be free from jealousy and envy of others.

Acknowledge and accept God's absolute, unconditional love.

"But God demonstrates his own love for us in this: While we were still sinners, Christ died for us."

(Romans 5:8)

If you want to have true self-dignity and self-esteem, you must first accept the unconditional love God offers you. To be loved by God is not dependent on our good and righteous deeds, but because God himself is love. God's love is absolute and unconditional.

"Whoever does not love does not know God, because God is love."

(1 John 4:8)

One thing God wants from us is to open ourselves up so that He can pour out His love in our hearts. Why is it difficult for us to accept the absolute unconditional love of God? We tend to think that God's love is conditional, because human love is conditional. Therefore, we must always keep in mind the truth of God's word.

"For God so loved the world that he gave his one and only Son, that whoever believes in him shall not perish but have eternal life."

(John 3:16)

God wants us to accept His love without any conditions. In response to His love, we will desire to worship Him, praise Him, and give Him thanks for who He is and what He has done for us.

When we know that we are God's unique and precious creation, we discover the value of our own existence. When we have an accurate understanding of ourselves and God's purpose for us then we can truly live a rewarding and valuable life.

"For I know the plans I have for you, declares the Lord, plans to prosper you and not to harm you, plans to give you hope and a future. Then you will call on me and come and pray to me, and I will listen to you. You will seek me and find me when you seek me with all your heart."

(Jeremiah 29:11-13)

CHAPTER 13

USEFUL GUIDELINES FOR INNER HEALING MINISTERS[5]

The steps listed below are basic guidelines for inner healing ministers to use during inner healing prayer. Each step is founded on a dialogue between the participant receiving ministry and the Lord, while the one facilitating the ministry is there to ask questions that will help guide the session. Prayer ministers must remember that their role is to help those receiving ministry to hear and receive from the Lord. Minister never lead, guide, direct, or interpret.

The following steps will help build trust between the Minister and the participant receiving inner healing ministry. Trust will enable the one receiving ministry to express their emotions and reveal their deep-seated soul wounds.

Inner Healing Ministry

Negative memories contain painful emotions and feelings that the enemy uses against us. God desires to heal us from this pain and set us free so we can be the person He has called us to be.

1. Ask the essential question: "Do you want the Lord to heal you?"
2. Have the participant close their eyes in order to prevent any distraction.
3. Facilitators then pray out loud for the participants. "Lord, I thank You that (name of participant(s)) wants to be free from the deception of satan and to be healed of the soul wounds. Lord, I thank You that You are here with us today and You

---

[5] Drs. Jerry and Sherill Piscopo have given permission to use the reference material in this chapter.

promise to never leave us or abandon us. We depend on Your great power to destroy satan's power to "kill, steal, and destroy." You have come to give us the abundant life, and (name of participant) wants Your abundant life. In Jesus' name, I bind all evil spirits from interfering or obstructing this healing process. Lord, I ask that no evil spirit will have any room to maneuver in today's healing process. I ask that You help (name of participant) bring all emotions and memories from within so that they may be healed and made whole again."

4. Have the participant pray out loud for the Lord's guidance for His healing.
5. Have the participant share the first memory that the Lord has shown them (regardless of how insignificant it may seem or even if the person does not fully understand its significance.)
6. Record what the participant says.
7. Record the emotions of the participant, not your own ideas or observations.
8. Have the participant carefully examine this memory, and express all feelings and emotions associated with it.
9. Have the participant to share what the Lord has shown him/her and record it.
10. Have the participant ask the Lord to show them the source of their negative feelings and emotions. Note: This is typically a belief or mindset that goes contrary to the Word of God, i.e., "I feel unloved. I feel rejected."
11. Have the participant to share what the Lord has shown them and record it.
12. Have the participant confirm their emotions and feelings, and record what they say.
13. Have the participant ask the Lord to clearly show them where these emotions and feelings are coming from, and record it.
14. If the participant needs to forgive someone, guide them through a prayer of forgiveness. If there is anything the participant needs to be forgiven for, guide them through a prayer for forgiveness.
15. Sever all ties to any and all curses and vows that the participant may have spoken towards themselves or others.
16. Have the participant renounce all yokes, bondages, and strongholds that the Lord has shown them, i.e., they are in bondage to critical thinking. They are yoked to an ungodly soul tie. There is a stronghold of alcohol in their family history.
17. Have the participant ask God for His truth regarding the memory He has shown them, i.e., "Your mom said she didn't love you because she was mad at your dad, and took it out on you."

18. Have the participant share what he has seen and felt.
19. Have the participant ask, "Lord, are there any other memories that I must know about?" If so, repeat the above steps.
20. After the participant is at peace with their memory or memories, pray a prayer of blessing over them, then seal shut any open doors through the blood of Jesus.

If necessary, for deeper healing, ask the following questions:

1. When was the most miserable and depressing time in your life?
2. How old were you?
3. What happened?
4. How did that make you feel?
5. Guide the participant to hear what the Lord says about this incident. After they feel the presence of the Lord, guide the participant through the following steps:
   - Have the participant pray, asking for the Lord's truth while examining the painful memory.
   - Have the participant ask the Lord why the incident happened.
   - Ask the participant to forgive everyone involved, including the participant and God.
   - Have the participant repent and renounce any self-judgment and negative beliefs about themselves.
   - Have the participant sever all ties from the inner vows they made about this incident.
   - Have the participant renounce negative words that have come back as a curse. (i.e., if your father was a violent alcoholic, you might have vowed never to drink or let anyone hurt you. If you saw your parents fight a lot, you probably vowed never to get married, or not to have children if you were to marry.)
   - Have the participant say the prayer of blessing for all those who have hurt them.
   - Pray to confirm their healing and have the participant repeat the prayer. Say a short prayer proclaiming that the power and influence of satan has now ceased, and to seal the participant's memory or memories in the blood of Jesus. Have the participant repeat that prayer.

If necessary for further ministry, ask these questions and repeat the steps outline above:

- What was the loneliest time in your life?
- What was the most humiliating time in your life?
- When did you experience the worst rejection in your life?
- When did you become the angriest in your life?

CHAPTER 14

USEFUL GUIDELINES FOR MINISTERING DELIVERANCE[6]

Purpose: To effectively lead a successful deliverance ministry.

The need for deliverance ministry

In contrast to the general belief, evil spirits do exist. The foundation of our faith is the teachings of the Bible. Angels and demons have never stopped working, even to this day.

> *"Are not all angels ministering spirits sent to serve those who will inherit salvation?"*
>
> (Hebrews 1:14)

> *"Finally, be strong in the Lord and in his mighty power.[1] Put on the full armor of God, so that you can take your stand against the devil's schemes. For our struggle is not against flesh and blood, but against the rulers, against the authorities, against the powers of this dark world and against the spiritual forces of evil in the heavenly realms."*
>
> (Ephesians 6:10-12)

> *"We know that we are children of God, and that the whole world is under the control of the evil one."*
>
> (1 John 5:19)

---

[6] Drs. Jerry and Sherill Piscopo have given permission to use the reference material in this chapter.

Satan falsely proclaims spiritual warfare and deliverance ministry as fantasies. However, Jesus is the only legitimate model of deliverance from evil spirits, and He lived a real life on this earth.

Challenges of the modern world

While the Holy Spirit has been very active, so has satan.

Many are walking in the path of destruction because of satan's efforts. We must remain active in fulfilling our mission in all areas in order to help those who wish to enter into the Lord's Kingdom.

Who must fulfill this ministry?

We are God's people for this age. This ministry falls on us and is a part of what we must do as believers for the Body of Christ.

> *"So Christ himself gave the apostles, the prophets, the evangelists, the pastors and teachers, to equip his people for works of service, so that the body of Christ may be built up."*
>
> (Ephesians 4:11-12)

> *"And these signs will accompany those who believe: In my name they will drive out demons; they will speak in new tongues;"*
>
> (Mark 16:17)

What must we pursue in deliverance ministry?

We must recognize the work and attacks of evil spirits and drive them out of people, so they can become those who the Lord has freed through His blood.

What must we prepare?

- We must first clearly identify the Lord is victorious.
- We must engrave the Word of God in our minds, declaring the Lord's complete victory and the power of His blood.
- We must know our enemies. A great ward commander knows their enemies well.

> *"having canceled the charge of our legal indebtedness, which stood against us and condemned us; he has taken it away, nailing it to the cross. And having disarmed the powers and authorities, he made a public spectacle of them, triumphing over them by the cross."*
>
> (Colossians 2:14-15)

> *"in order that satan might not outwit us. For we are not unaware of his schemes."*
>
> (2 Corinthians 2:11)

We must know what our weapons are and understand how to use them

- The name of the Lord.
- The blood of Jesus.
- The Word of God.
- The gifts of the Holy Spirit.
- Understand our position and authority over the enemy as members of the Body of Christ.
- We must fully understand our limitations without the power of the Holy Spirit.
- We must remain spiritually awake so that we walk in obedience to the Lord.
- We must learn from those who are experienced in spiritual warfare and work with them.

Our enemy

The kingdom of darkness is extremely well organized. Demons, or evil spirits, are all under the same leadership: satan. It is not appropriate for Christians to say of another Christian, "a person possessed by demons." The correct expression is "a person under the influence of a demon."

What is a demon?

A demon is a shapeless evil spirit that wants to enter into the body and minds of a person to gain full control of them. Demons have their own unique characteristics. Demons have a will, as well as power, knowledge, self-awareness, perception, and the ability to speak. The kingdom of satan is very well organized, with a chain of command and specialized talent levels that are well defined, as per a military organization.

> *"For our struggle is not against flesh and blood, but against the rulers, against the authorities, against the powers of this dark world and against the spiritual forces of evil in the heavenly realms."*
>
> (Ephesians 6:12)

Demons are inferior beings to angels. Some demons are much more powerful than others.

> *"Then it goes and takes with it seven other spirits more wicked than itself, and they go in and live there. And the final condition of that person is worse than the first. That is how it will be with this wicked generation."*
>
> (Matthew 12:45)

> *"In fact, no one can enter a strong man's house without first tying him up. Then he can plunder the strong man's house."*
>
> (Mark 3:27)

How demons operate

Demons are under satan's control and direction.

> *"But when the Pharisees heard this, they said, "It is only by Beelzebub, the prince of demons, that this fellow drives out demons."*
>
> (Matthew 12:24)

Demons exercise their "influence" outside of a human body, but "control" the individual when inside the body. Demons tempt, deceive, enslave, cause pain, and drive us to sin. Demons want all of humankind to self-destruct morally, spiritually, physically, and mentally. Because God loves us, demons hate us.

How can you tell someone needs deliverance ministry?

The power of the Holy Spirit exposes demons. The problems caused by demons are of a wide variety, and any symptoms do not improve through medicine or therapies. Demons cause emotional problems, psychological problems, sexual problems, addictions, all types of illnesses, religious trial and errors, and the list goes on.

Demons often operate in groups. The Bible speaks of "a strong man" and which implies that there are followers operating with him.

> *"In fact, no one can enter a strong man's house without first tying him up. Then he can plunder the strong man's house."*
>
> (Mark 3:27)

Would it be wise for us to tell someone they need deliverance?

Whether you tell someone about deliverance depends on each individual and on your relationship with them. A personal testimony or teaching about what the Word of God says regarding deliverance will encourage the person to participate. You must always follow the Holy Spirit as to the appropriate timing.

The participant's attitude is more important than anything. They must have a willing heart to seek help, a cooperative attitude, strong confidence in the Word and the Holy Spirit, and who is providing the deliverance ministry.

CHAPTER 15

DEMON POSSESSION AND CHRISTIANS[7]

Through inner healing ministry, we learn how to identify the root of a problem and appropriate treatment for it. Is it possible for Christians to be under the influence of a demon? It most certainly is. The argument against a Christian under a demon's influence is caused by misunderstanding about the phrase "possessed by demons" in the Bible.

What does it mean to be "possessed by a demon"? The Greek definition is to be *oppressed* by an evil spirit. Let's be clear: There is no mention of a demon having an absolute ownership and control over a born-again believer in the Bible.

Christians can suffer from the oppressive influence of an evil spirit. However, this can happen in the domain of the body and soul, but not in a Christian's spirit. An evil spirit dwelling in a man's body and soul realm does not always leave just because the person becomes a born-again Christian. Our spirit is born again, but the body and soul are in a continual need of healing.

> *"Therefore, since we have these promises, dear friends, let us purify ourselves from everything that contaminates body and spirit, perfecting holiness out of reverence for God."*
>
> (2 Corinthians 7:1)

According to the Bible, even after one becomes a born-again Christian there may be a need for healing in the realm of the soul (mind, will, and emotions).

---

[7] Permission to use reference material in this chapter from Drs. Jerry and Sherill Piscopo.

"Create in me a pure heart, O God, and renew a steadfast spirit within me."
(Psalms 51:10)

We need to be cleansed, healed, and liberated from demonic influence, including yokes, bondages, and strongholds. Many Christians blame their problems on the devil instead of admitting and owning their choices and actions, and choosing to follow fleshly desires and sins.

Deliverance ministry is focused on driving out the demon, evil spirit, that has penetrated an individual's body and soul, and is working through them. Once a demon has been driven out, it will seek to return (see Luke 11:24). It is the individual's responsibility to maintain their freedom through a pure and steadfast heart.

We can confront the wounds of the past through inner healing ministry. We can also receive freedom from the oppression of an evil spirit through deliverance. However, we must choose to change our attitude, response, lifestyle, habits, and align our will to serve God. If we do not make any changes, we can end up suffering through even stronger oppression and even more painful wounds. Even when inner healing ministry and deliverance are successful, they will only provide temporary relief unless there are certain changes in specific areas of our life. However, we must remember that only those who rely on the help of the Holy Spirit can change these important areas.

Should inner healing prayer come first or deliverance ministry? Inner healing should come first to give understanding as to why and how emotional bondages are connected to our wounded souls through painful memories. After inner healing, many evil spirits will be exposed. Inner healing takes away the legal ground that the spirits use to bring oppression. Deliverance will be more effective after the painful memories and emotional wounds are healed.

When an evil spirit is driven out, it will quickly return unless the root of the emotional wound receives a complete healing. As we are healed in our body, soul, and spirit, we will be cleansed by the blood of Christ. God's will towards us is to be healed so that we can grow in spiritual maturity and Christ likeness.

CHAPTER 16

HOW TO MAINTAIN INNER HEALING AND DELIVERANCE[8]

Live a life of prayer and make every decision through a prayer

- Pray continually in the Holy Spirit. (1 Thessalonians 5:17)
- Stay in the presence of the Lord. (Psalms 16:11)
- Have fellowship with the Lord. (1 John 1:3)
- Put on the full armor of God, arm yourself with prayer and Scripture. (Ephesians 6:10-18)
- Praise and prayer expressing your thanksgiving respect and joy for God will silence our foes. (Psalms 8:2)

Daily eat your spiritual food for your spiritual survival (2 Peter 2:2)

- Read, study, and meditate on the Word of God daily. (Joshua 1:8)
- As Jesus did, we defeat satan with the Word of God. (Luke 4)
- The Word of God shines a light upon our soul. (James 1:22-25)
- The Word of God is a lamp on our feet, a light on our path. (Psalms 119:105)
- The Word of God cleanses us. (Ephesians 5:25-26)
- The Word of God is a sword. (Hebrews 4:12)
- No blessing is possible without the Word of God. It is important to read the Bible and to memorize Bible verses.

---

[8] Permission to use reference material in this chapter from Drs. Jerry and Sherill Piscopo.

Always praise the Lord and in all circumstances with a thankful attitude (Mark 11:23)

- Positive attitude and confession are an expression of faith.
- Do not make negative confessions.
- Negative confessions are a demon's influence.
- Praise God in all things, including when you are faced with a problem. (Ephesians 5:20, Hebrews 13:15-16)

Make a commitment to the Lord everyday (Galatians 5:19-21, 24, Ephesians 5:15-17; Philippians 4:8-9)

- Seek the Lord's guidance and wisdom.
- Stop your old habits that do not give glory to the Lord.
- Deny desires of your body and bring them to the cross. (Romans 6:12-13; James 47-10)
- Develop the fruit of the Spirit in your life. (Galatians 5:22-34)

Put the Lord first in all things and devote yourself to the Lord (Ephesians 6:16)

- The Lord does not like compromise. Fill your life with things that glorify the Lord and show His character through your words, your actions, and your thoughts.

Stand firm against satan (Matthew 12:29; 16:19; 18:18)

- When satan attacks you, crush him with the power of the name of Jesus Christ.

Attend a church filled with the Holy Spirit and participate in the meetings (1 Corinthians 12:7-14)

- Find your place within a local Church and do what is required of you.
- Seek the gifts of the Holy Spirit and use them within and outside the Church.
- Obey those in authority.

Have a partner in prayer

- We all need a prayer partner with whom we can share not only the burden in our heart but joyful things.
- Things shared between prayer partners must remain confidential.

Allow God to heal your inner being

- Inner Healing is maintained through a daily relationship with the Lord.

Make forgiveness a part of your life

- Work hard to always forgive quickly, and never allow bitterness in your life.
- Learn how to live a holy life through the Holy Spirit. (1 John 2:27)
- Guard your thoughts. (2 Corinthians 10:3-5)
- Guard your tongue. (1 Peter 4:11; Ephesians 5:2)
- Allow the Holy Spirit to change you as the Lord desires (Titus 3:5) and always fill your house with the Holy Spirit.

Learn how to live a holy life through the Holy Spirit (1 John 2:27)

- Guard your thoughts. (2 Corinthians 10:3-5)
- Guard your tongue. (1 Peter 4:11; Ephesians 5:2)
- Allow the Holy Spirit to change you as the Lord desires (Titus 3:5) and always fill your "house" (your body) with the Holy Spirit.

Practice always depending on the blood of Jesus

- To depend on the blood of Jesus is to declare our right as a believer to be protected from all things evil. (Revelation 12:10-11)

Avoid all kinds of deception

- Avoid such things as superstition, psychic healing, witchcraft, fortune telling, sorcery etc. at all costs. (Deuteronomy 18:9-13)

Distance yourself from all cults

- Mormonism, Islam, Unitarian, Jehovah's Witness, etc.

Establish a good relationship with your neighbors
(Colossians 3:15-17)

Have a fellowship with your fellow brothers and sisters in Christ, and avoid *evil* associations with unbelievers. Note: this does not mean that you cannot fellowship with unbelievers, but to be aware of any evil that may be present.

The above principles will help you maintain your healing and deliverance. Demons can never enter a "house" filled with holiness, where Jesus is Lord.

Jesus has made perfect blessing possible and wants us to reside in the freedom His blessings provide. We must continue pursuing more freedom in the Lord (Romans 5:10).

If you need further help, feel free to contact Sunshine International Ministries.

A NOTE TO MY READERS

Congratulations! I am so proud of you for completing this workbook.

You have gone through an extensive teaching on inner healing and deliverance. If you apply this information to your life on a daily basis, you will see yourself change and grow in ways you've never imagined. Why? Because you are allowing the Holy Spirit to do a deep work in your soul and bring you freedom from the yokes, strongholds, and bondages that have been holding you back in your mind, will, and emotions.

Jesus came to set the captive free (see Isaiah 61:1; Luke 4:18-19). He also said the truth will set you free (see John 8:32). When you allow the Holy Spirit to bring you His truth according to biblical principles, freedom will flood your soul. And the more freedom you experience, the greater love you will have for Jesus and the people He brings into your life.

I encourage you to go through this workbook as many times as needed, so that you receive all that God has for you.

In closing, I speak these words over you:

> *"Grace and peace be yours in abundance through the knowledge of God and of Jesus our Lord."*
>
> (2 Peter 1:2)

Your sister in Christ,
Dr. Sun Fannin

ACKNOWLEDGEMENTS

It truly is by the grace of God that I can publish my first workbook in my teaching series under the title *Inner Healing Deliverance & Restoration: A Workbook for the Spiritually Broken*. This is a vision the Lord gave me several years ago, and I'm grateful to the Lord for giving me His blessing to publish it. I am excited about this teaching series!

I sincerely give thanks and glory to God for equipping me. I have used these notes in countless seminars and training sessions in many churches and Sunshine Ministries Seminars for many years.

I would like to thank my late husband, Pastor Larry who always believed in me and supported me.

I am so appreciative of the late Dr. Jerry Piscopo, who faithfully served as Senior Pastor of Evangel Church Roseville, Michigan and Overseer of Evangel Association of Churches and Ministries (EACM), and Dr. Sherrill Piscopo who continues to lead in both roles as my mentor and overseer. I appreciate you and love you so much!

Thank you Simon Presland for all of your hard work. This would not have been created without you!

Finally, I want to thank my readers with all my heart! You will experience inner healing, deliverance, and restoration through this workbook, and I cannot wait to hear your testimonies!

In the faithful and everlasting love of Christ,
Dr. Sun Fannin,
Overseer and Co-Pastor of Evangel Christian Church Greenfield Indiana,
and Founder of Sunshine International Ministries

ABOUT THE AUTHOR

Dr. Sun Fannin was born and raised in South Korea and came to the United States in 1972. In 1981, she and her late husband, Dr. Larry Fannin, founded and co-pastored Evangel Christian Church in Greenfield, Indiana for 37 years until his passing. In 2018, after raising up their oldest son, Pastor Jody, to become senior pastor, she is now the overseer of Evangel.

In 1985, Pastor Sun established Sunshine International Ministries (SIM). She has led countless prayer meetings, seminars, and conferences on such diverse topics as prayer and intercession, school of prophecy, inner healing, deliverance and restoration, and leadership training seminars. Pastor Sun has also organized a nationwide, inter-denominational prayer network for America's revival. Since 2002, she has been an Overseer of the Asian Region for Evangel Association of Churches and Ministries (EACM), while expanding her ministry throughout the U.S. and Asia to fulfill her mission as an Apostle and Prophet.

Dr. Sun's life and ministry has been made into documentary programs by two Christian TV stations in the U.S., both of which have been aired on multiple occasions. In 1999, she received a Certificate of Appreciation from the mayor of Greenfield for more than 20 years of exemplary community service performed on behalf of the Samaritans of the area. In 2000, the Indianapolis Star ran a front-page article about Dr. Sun in its Religion Section and introduced her as a special servant of God and a vessel used by God to bless our society.

Dr. Sun is the author of: *The Bad Luck Baby* (her autobiography); *If My People* (a book about fasting and prayer); *This Too Will Pass* (continuation of her autobiography); *Inner Healing Deliverance & Restoration: A Workbook for the Spiritually Broken*; and *Intercessory Prayer: The Vital Link Between Heaven and Earth*. All books have been published in multiple languages.

In January 2005, Dr. Sun received an Honorary Doctorate Degree in Theology from Destiny Christian University, Florida.

Dr. Sun is a member of EACM (Evangel Associations of Churches and Ministries) and is the director of the Asian region for EACM. She was a lecturer and a professor at Destiny School of Ministry under the late Dr. Jerry Piscopo's leadership and is currently working in the same capacity at Agape Seminary of Seoul, Korea, led by Chancellor Rev. Tae Jin Kim.